The Golden Hour

1 Hour a Day to Grow Your Gym Forever

Chris Cooper

Two-Brain Business

Two-Brain Business

THE GOLDEN HOUR
1 Hour a Day to Grow Your Gym Forever
By Chris Cooper

Copyright © 2024 Two-Brain Business Inc.
All rights reserved.

ISBN 9798338762127

This is more than a book: it's a prescription for daily action. To make those actions easier, I've included step-by-step instructions in this book. I've also recorded videos to help you.

Watch the videos by scanning this QR code below, or visit

WWW.GOLDENHOURCHALLENGE.COM

CONTENTS

Introduction 1

How the Golden Hour Helped Me Escape Failure 6

The Golden Hour Millionaires and the Key to Their Success 14

Designing the Golden Hour 23

    G—Go to a Place Where You Can Focus 31
    O—Open Your Mind 34
    L—Lead with Marketing "Reps" 36
    D—Do Your Big Projects 38
    E—End After One Hour 41
    N—Next Steps 43

The Six-Week Golden Hour Challenge 45

The Four Phases of Golden Hour Success 89

    Phase 1—Practicing focus 90
    Phase 2—Creating and Stacking Habits 95
    Phase 3—Maintaining Momentum 100
    Phase 4—Turn Habits Into Skills 107

The Golden Hour LITE—the Truth About Productivity 116

Fulfilling the Golden Age 120

Appendix 1: How to Publish a Blog Post or Quickcast 130
Appendix 2: How to Distribute Your Content 145
Appendix 3: How to Check In With Your Clients 153
Appendix 4: How to Mine Your Leads 155
Appendix 5: How to Set Up Your Social Media Calendar 162
Appendix 6: How to Spotlight Your Clients 172
Appendix 7: How to Send a Weekly Preview To Your Staff 174

INTRODUCTION

"Every day, do one thing to grow your business before you do anything else."

The first 60 minutes of your day can transform your business and your life.

The first hour of your day is golden: you're more focused, less distracted and less interrupted than at any other time.

Using that "Golden Hour" to build your gym will get you more clients, create better opportunities for your staff and make you more money. As a bonus, you'll wind up working LESS overall.

As a hard-working gym owner, you're used to getting up early. You might even already have a series of "morning habits" you perform to improve your fitness or mindset.

You might already understand that if you want to improve any area of your life, you do it first thing in the morning, before you do anything else.

And if someone asked you "How do I improve my fitness?" you might tell them to start their day with exercise, or preparing their meals in advance.

But what if your goal is to grow your fitness business? What do you DO in that time?

In this book, I'll tell you exactly what to do in your Golden Hour. I'll share what the fastest-growing gyms in the largest gym mentorship practice in the world do. I'm even going to give you step-by-step instructions to get you started.

These successful gyms don't do the same thing every single morning. But they have basic habits that they repeat every seven days. The habits take about 15 minutes each, and keep their gyms growing and growing—even to the point of making the gym owner a millionaire.

I know: it sounds too easy. And most business books love to make business sound easy. But if you've been reading along with me for the last decade, you know that I share the struggles, the hardships—and the solutions—with full transparency.

When I adopted the Golden Hour strategy, I turned my failing gym into a successful one. And it's been key to helping more than 50 other gym owners become millionaires through our mentorship practice, Two-Brain Business, in the last three years.

The Gym Was Running Me

Of course, gym owners are used to starting the day early compared to most other people. But it's not about what time you start. It's about what you do with the time.

If you don't master the Golden Hour and learn how to use that time well, you will be at the mercy of events for the rest of the day.

I know what it's like.

Every day, you get up early and head to the gym. It's probably still dark when you get there.

You go through the ritual of opening up: flicking on the lights, checking the bathrooms, lighting up the sign, unlocking the door.

You paint a smile on your face to greet the first clients—the ones who show up 15 minutes before class. You're thinking "They're too early, I'm not ready..."

You start the session on time—maybe it's a class, maybe it's 1:1 personal training. You do as you always do. You pour all your energy into the class, all your care into the clients.

Then you do it again the next hour. By the time most people head out to work, you've already been going full out for three hours.

This continues throughout the day. By late afternoon, you're physically and mentally exhausted, but you're staring down several more hours of coaching before you head home.

The late afternoon and evening are an exercise in resilience. You're digging into your own mental reserves and struggling to stay focused on the client in front of you instead of your unpaid bills, late staff, and the bathroom you'll have to clean at 9pm before you can leave.

And as you lie down in bed, exhausted and frustrated, the thought overriding everything else is the worst thought of all: "It's not going to be any different tomorrow."

Maybe all of this rings true for you; maybe just parts of it.

This was my typical day for over a decade as a gym owner. And the real blow came when I read this in a book:

"Most business owners who make it to the end of their first decade don't have ten years of experience. They have one year of experience, repeated ten times."

That really stuck with me. I was stuck on 'repeat', just living the same day over and over, and running out of time. My business wasn't growing and neither was I. The business was staying the same because I was staying the same.

Getting Out of the Rut

I knew I had to find a way to get out of that rut and I was able to do that.

First, I started reading books about business instead of books about coaching. I listened to audiobooks for about an hour every day. I got some great ideas—but I didn't act on any of them. My business didn't change even though I knew more.

Then I got a mentor. He told me what to do first. I did it, and the business changed... but I was doing his assignments all weekend or getting up at 4am to do them.

Don't get me wrong: they saved my business. But adding more hours to the day wasn't sustainable.

Things changed when I shared this with my mentor. He told me something that changed my life: "Chris, NEVER COACH THE MORNING CLASS!" I'll share more of that story with you later.

But the key to fixing my business, growing my business, and then building a huge worldwide movement was mastering the Golden Hour.

Those first 60 minutes of the day can be the difference between continuing to have days like I've just described and living life on your own terms.

My mantra for the Golden Hour is that statement you see at the start of this segment: *"Every day, do one thing to grow your business before you do anything else."*

The Golden Hour

There are a lot of things you *could* do to grow your business, and mentors make those things clearer. But if you don't get the work done, nothing will change.

So how do you get the work done? The key to that is the Golden Hour.

You set aside one hour, every day, to work ON your business instead of working IN it.

This means you do the things that attract new clients, improve your service and keep clients around longer. It means you build operational processes that save you time and elevate your service delivery. It means you can build staff ascension models and opportunities to make real careers for other people... IF you set aside the time to do it.

And if you set aside your FIRST hour every day, then you're devoting your BEST, most focused time to growing your business.

In this book, I'm going to teach you how to master the Golden Hour.

First let me tell you the rest of the story.

HOW THE GOLDEN HOUR HELPED ME ESCAPE FAILURE

Here's the full story of how the Golden Hour developed: In 2009, I was almost bankrupt.

I hadn't been paid in two weeks, and didn't know how we were going to buy groceries.

My clients owed me about $12,000—but I didn't have $200 in the bank, and my staff were due to be paid in three days.

It was August 19, and I knew we couldn't pay the rent for September, let alone the city tax bill that was sitting on my desk.

It was late afternoon, and I was sitting on a park bench across the street from my gym. It was hot, and I was sweating through my black collared polo.

I was in the pit of despair: I was working 16 hours every day. I was listening to every business audiobook and reading every article about training I could find.

I had a grocery list of certifications after my name. My clients were getting good results. My trainers were making more per hour than they could make anywhere else in town. And we were failing. The dream was ending.

The worst part, for me, was that I just couldn't figure out "the answer" to business. I knew I was a better trainer than the others in town (who all appeared to be killing it.) My prices were the same as theirs. And I was working harder than anyone I knew. But I'd run out of money and run out of time.

I had no idea what to do. So I just sat there and sweated.

If there was a price to be paid for success, I'd have paid it. But I couldn't see a path forward: just another thirty years of missing my kids and wife, making the same small-talk conversations with the 43 clients I trained every week, losing sleep over money and stressing about the water bill.

I was already reading the 'help wanted' ads in the online newspapers and skipping lunch to save money. I couldn't work any harder (and didn't want to) but would have tried to if that would have made a difference.

I couldn't find a single example of a personal trainer who wasn't working a 60-hour week, or barely making ends meet. In fact, I couldn't find a single example of a personal trainer who stuck with the business for ten years, let alone thirty!

The Phone Was Ringing...

After an hour of sweating in the sun, I wasn't feeling any better—but I got up off the bench because I had yet another client appointment. Now I was staring down six training sessions in a row—and I hadn't eaten lunch. Even on a daily level, things were getting worse.

I walked across the street and clanged my way up the rear fire escape to our second-floor studio. The phone was ringing, so I ran down the hall to answer it—maybe this was a new client who wanted to pay me for training?

Instead, it was a friend who worked at the local business innovation center. I was barely paying attention as he gave me some news: a local CEO who had pulled off a massive turnaround was cashing out and leaving town. But before he did, he was going to mentor five local entrepreneurs as a legacy project.

I didn't see how this could help—and I knew it would take up more of my time, which was completely maxed out—but I couldn't figure out how to turn my friend down. He was excited about the opportunity for me. So I agreed to take it, knowing that I didn't have the time OR the money to participate.

The mentorship program taught me a lot about business. But more importantly, it helped me build a new skill: the ability to FOCUS and get the RIGHT work DONE, when I set myself up for success properly.

Here's what happened:

I took the first meeting with my new mentor, Denis Turcotte. We sat in a borrowed office for two hours, going through my long-term goals and breaking down what I needed from the gym. I'd never done that before, but the goals seemed SO distant that I wasn't confident that I'd ever get there, and I couldn't see the steps from where I currently sat to that ideal spot.

After two hours, we wrapped up and I said, "Thanks. What do I owe for the session?"

I was terrified: my bank account was still empty, and the check that was in my pocket would probably bounce.

He said, "Five hundred dollars."

I tried to look nonchalant, but I knew there was NO WAY I could cover that check.

I was also a bit embarrassed that the check was damp—I was sweating from the hard mental workout he'd just given me. But that was the least of my concerns.

Don't Cash That Check

I let him put the check in his pocket, and then I shook his hand and drove away. But I was riddled with guilt all the way back to the gym. When I arrived, I went straight to the phone and called Denis.

"Can you hold onto that check?" I asked. "I won't have the money to cover it until next week sometime."

Denis' response shocked me. He said, "No."

Then he continued: "What we covered today is enough to make you $500 by Monday. If I cash the check tomorrow (a Friday), the money will be in your account... if you do what I told you. If you don't, the check will bounce and our relationship will come to an end. Okay?"

He didn't say it unkindly, but the message was clear: I really didn't have a choice.

And so, back to the wall, I spent Friday asking clients if they'd like to buy 10 or 20 PT sessions in advance, instead of being billed at the end of the month as they usually were.

One client—Bob, a real estate agent—said, "Sure." He probably knew why I was asking. But that dropped $495 into my account immediately.

The fear of bouncing that check to Denis forced me to focus on doing the ONE thing required to make more money—no matter how uncomfortable I was asking other people to pay in advance (or at all, which was part of my problem.)

Denis knew how to get me to focus on the most important thing. But he also knew how to get me to act on it. In this case, the pain of taking action was less than the pain of embarrassment when that check bounced.

The check cleared on Monday, and I booked my next appointment with Denis.

Eager to make even more money, I left that appointment with a clear action step: hire a cleaner to buy back three hours of time per week, then reinvest those hours into marketing to my email list. I very quickly sold another personal training package. I was starting to feel great momentum. I booked my third appointment for mentorship.

The Big Task

This time, our conversation took a different direction. Denis told me that I had to write a staff handbook for every single thing that happened in my business. He had me listen to "The E-Myth" book, and then do the work assigned by the author.

I was eager to get this project behind me, but it was a big one—and boring as hell. I can remember sitting at my coffee table for hours—an entire weekend, really—and writing out every mundane task in my gym, step by step. I got most of it done, but by Sunday afternoon I was mentally spent. I could no longer focus on the work, and chose to take my kids to the park instead.

Monday came and went—I didn't finish the playbook.

Soon it was Friday, and it still wasn't done.

I told myself, "I just have a bit more to finish... I'll wait until Monday."

On Monday, Denis' secretary called to ask why I hadn't booked my fourth appointment. Denis was headed out of town on holiday. I said, "I'll book one when he's back." So we chose a spot two weeks in the future.

You know what happened next: I procrastinated on that staff handbook until the night before my appointment with Denis, then I got it done.

At our next appointment, we moved on to another operational task: creating a hiring chart and "roles" from all the tasks I'd outlined. I was getting impatient. I asked "When are we going to get to the marketing?"

He said, "You're not ready for marketing. Your operations aren't good enough. If you attract people right now, they'll quit and never come back. Get your operations dialed before you start bringing more people in."

I was impatient, but trusted Denis.

That's when he said, "We only have one more appointment together. We'll talk about marketing then... but I don't want to do it until you have the operational work done."

Oh, shit!

Preparing to Fly Solo

I quickly realized that I was going to have to learn to fly solo eventually; that if I didn't do the work, I'd have wasted this brief opportunity; and that I was at risk of falling "off the wagon" as soon as Denis was gone.

I didn't want to lose my momentum, and I really didn't want to forget the lessons he'd taught me and go back to my former failure.

Luckily, I remembered my skill of Focus.

When I was in college, I picked up the Feynman Technique for learning. The important part was this: if you teach a concept to someone else, you'll remember it better.

When I was studying for my CSCS certification at the end of my degree, I set up a kids' plastic chalkboard in my kitchen, and taught exercise science theory to my coffee pot and dishware.

It worked: I recalled a lot of that text and absolutely smashed the exam, which was regarded as the hardest in the field at the time.

Remembering the Feynman technique, I said, "OK Chris, you need to write all of this down so you remember it." But I had no one to teach it to—I didn't know many other gym owners, and thought the other local gym owners were my 'competition'.

So I decided to teach it all to "Future Chris": I'd write down everything Denis taught me, step by step, and create a business resource that I could read again in the future.

I was reading Seth Godin at the time. He was a fan of TypePad. I signed up for TypePad and registered a blog. I called it "DontBuyAds" as a reminder to myself that I wasn't ready for marketing yet. And I started writing letters to Future Chris.

Every day, I would start by writing myself a note:

1. What I'd accomplished the day before.

2. What I'd just learned from an audiobook on my commute.

3. Notes for the future, including lessons and MANY mistakes. (*"Dear Chris, don't ever screw THIS up again!"* and *"Well, I screwed this up. Here's how I'll do it next time."*)

I didn't realize it, but I was actually learning to meditate. The written blog post was really just me looking at my thoughts.

There was no such thing as a private blog back then, so DontBuyAds was public from the start. And as I wrote my daily love letters to "Future Chris", other gym owners found them and started to read them.

I kept the blog up, because some of the posts *were* useful, but there was also a lot of fluff in there. Some of the posts were summaries of books I'd just finished; some were extremely useful templates that others asked to copy.

Skimming that blog now paints a picture of my mindset, though: right after a meeting with Denis or another mentor, I'd write something very important, actionable, and clear. Over time, the posts become more vague and less actionable... and then I'd meet with a mentor and regain clarity.

But simply writing in the blog was more than a reminder or a to-do list; it helped me maintain my daily focus, set aside an hour a day to work on the business, and organize my thoughts. And sharing my mistakes was also powerful for me (and my readers).

Public Commitment

There's an old story about Arnold Schwarzenegger as a teenager. Most of Arnold's muscles grew pretty quickly—he had a huge chest and arms by age 17. But his calves would never grow. They were little toothpicks. They embarrassed him. So he cut the lower legs off all his pants, so they were always visible. His transparency forced him to train his calves hard, every day, until they became the best part of his physique (in his words).

Placing my wins (and many failures) in the public eye had the same effect on me. I was embarrassed to share the mistakes—but I was more scared to repeat them. So I wrote them down.

"Every day, do one thing to grow your business before you do anything else" became my mantra nearly 20 years ago. I knew that if I could apply my BEST, most productive hour every day to growing my business, it couldn't help but grow.

Over time, writing became my morning meditation. It cleared the debris out of my head. The writing helped me focus my attention-deficit brain (so typical for an entrepreneur). When I finished writing for the day, I'd be clear-headed, calm, and know exactly what to do next.

That process—and the power of FOCUS—was the key to me turning my business around and, as we'll see in the next chapter, it became a successful model that others followed.

THE GOLDEN HOUR MILLIONAIRES AND THE KEY TO THEIR SUCCESS

Although I began following my Golden Hour each morning to help myself, it led to a process that has helped thousands of other gym owners, and several of them have become millionaires as a result.

When I started writing my blog at DontBuyAds.com, I was following the Feynman Technique, which—as I mentioned— is based on the idea that if you teach a concept to someone else, you'll remember it better.

It turned out that an additional benefit of doing this was that it acted as a form of meditation. That brain dump cleared my mind and readied it for intense focus.

At the start of this process in 2008, I was working 14 hours a day and nearly bankrupt. That's when I found my mentor.

Over the next four to five years, I was consistently doing my Golden Hour each day and my business improved.

At the same time, my blog posts sharing what I was doing were out there in public. Other gym owners started to follow them and what they learned from me led to them getting better results.

In 2012 I used some of the top posts from my blog as the basis for my first book "Two-Brain Business".

By the time the book was done, my gym had been fixed, I was making a good living, and working shorter and fewer days every week.

When I wrote that book, I thought I was sharing the strategies behind my success.

But I came to realize that it was actually the process of writing the blog and the book that led to my success.

Showing up at the gym every day a little earlier than necessary, I'd go into my office, lock the door, and write about what I did the day before, or what I was working on.

My morning habit forced me to take action—not just to acquire knowledge.

Writing every morning forced me to take action.

I slowly developed the habit of DOING.

Within a year of publication, the book became the best-selling fitness business book of all time.

That led to me starting to mentor other gym owners and in 2016, we officially launched Two-Brain Business as a mentorship practice with 13 clients on the first day.

By 2020, with nearly 1,000 gyms mentored, we partnered with industry software companies to compile data from 15,000 gyms around the world, and published it for free.

Today, we're the largest gym mentorship practice in the world, with over 1,000 current gyms in the program and more than 2,500 alumni.

WANTING SUCCESS FOR EVERYONE

Working with so many gym owners you start to learn about what makes some people more successful than others.

Because here's the thing...

- Every gym in our program has access to the same huge library of videos and resources and done-for-you templates and services.
- Every gym has a 1:1 mentor to clarify their goals, build them a plan and hold them to it. They all have access to the same high level of mentorship they can't get anywhere else.
- Every gym has the same initial two-week sprint with a few minor tweaks.
- Every gym has the same number of calls, they are in the same private Facebook groups and they are invited to the same weekly Office Hours.
- Every gym has the same caring client success team checking in on them.

This is the highest standard of mentorship in the world: our knowledge is backed by data and evidence; our mentors are experienced and caring and VERY good gym owners themselves. It's everything a gym owner could possibly need to be successful.

But still… some do better than others in our program.

How is that possible?

In 2023, I set out to find out why.

After speaking at our annual Summit event in Chicago, I returned home and dove straight into the data. I combed through our very deep set of records on every client.

I could see their revenues, client headcounts, retention rate, even how much the owner worked. I could go back years, in most cases. I could read the story of their business in their metrics. And I could do that for the 1,000 gyms in our program and our 2,000+ alumni, too.

Two months into this research, I was—well, I was pissed.

While nearly everyone got great results in our program, a small subset—about 8%—didn't.

The reason was obvious: they just didn't do the work.

There were missed meetings, distractions, unreturned emails, incompleted modules, unused resources and, sometimes, a frustrating exit. They gave up on themselves and didn't grow within our program.

The bright spot was that, at the other end of the spectrum, 12.5% of our clients had absolutely incredible results—they were going from broke gym owners to millionaires in three years or less.

One in eight people in our program weren't just turning their gyms around—they were reaching heights I hadn't even thought possible a decade before. And they were still going!

The rest of our clients—the other 80%—were in the middle. Most were getting really good results, but the top 12.5% were getting really incredible results. I wanted those results for everyone.

These numbers are actually consistent with data from academic studies on learning. But it wasn't good enough for me.

I want EVERY gym owner to be successful, especially those in our mentorship program. Anything less than complete success is frustrating for me—hell, it keeps me up at night.

So after ruminating on "what are the worst-performing gyms doing wrong?" for two months, I found a few things they had in common:

- **Distraction:** "I just don't have time to get this work done."
- **Overwhelm:** "I just have so much on my plate, I need to do X and Y before I can even think about Z..."
- **Burnout:** "I just don't feel like doing this. I want a quick solution or I'm going to give up."
- **Cynicism:** "I'm not doing that. Can't you make my business better without changing anything?"

Now, these people all signed up with the best of intentions.

They WANTED to save their business and be successful with mentorship—they were either out of time, out of patience or otherwise too far gone. They'd run out of runway.

And I didn't know how to fix it—yet. So I turned to the top 12.5% for answers.

Lessons from the Top 12.5%

These gyms told a remarkably different story.

The owners ascended rapidly through our program. They quickly found success—usually within the first few days. They reported their small wins right away, and asked "What's the next step?" They showed up for calls with their mentor on time, ready to work—and often ended the call early with a "Got it. I'll go work on this and tell you when I'm done." And then they did!

WIthin two years, one month and nine days, on average, they'd gone from a weak or failing gym to earning $100,000 per year in profit. Then most of them jumped into our higher-tier program, and within another year or so, had built a net worth of $1 million or more.

That's right: **Three years after starting, they were millionaires.** I even wrote a book about them (Millionaire Gym Owner) recording exactly what they'd done.

They were a pleasure to mentor. They did the work quickly. And when we invited them on to our podcast, or talked with them in person, they always said the exact same thing:

"I just did what my mentor told me," or *"I just followed the Two-Brain instructions exactly."*

Now every gym is slightly different, but with the same strategies, tactics, and tools tailored through 1:1 mentorship, the results should have been the same for all of them.

The Golden Hour Millionaires and the Key to Their Success

Why weren't they?

It took me another year to figure it out.

I had to read emails between the strong gyms and their mentor. I had to watch video recordings of the weaker gyms.

Slowly, bit by bit, the answer began to emerge.

These gym owners didn't just do what they were told. They did what they were told over and over and over again. They didn't stop doing what they were told.

Most entrepreneurs—including me—are always on the lookout for new things. We're attracted to novelty. We get excited by new ideas and can't wait to try them out. The problem is that, with limited time, we're always changing what we're doing. Instead of repeating the important stuff, we replace it with the new stuff.

The best gym owners in the world don't do that. They repeat, not replace. They answer text messages from leads at 8:34pm. They book regular goal reviews with their clients and don't skip them. They publish content every single Monday—not because they enjoy producing content, but because it's Monday.

The Key Difference

When I'd completed that exercise, I realized the standout difference was simply that the most successful gyms do what their mentor tells them.

But doesn't everyone? Everyone definitely SAYS they do the work their mentor tells them to do.

But I noticed that the most successful people do it FASTER.

For example, if a mentor tells a gym owner to raise their rates and they start working through the steps to do so, the successful ones have their rate increase letter, their staff briefing, and the other 10 things on our 'rate increase checklist' done within the month.

Others will talk about it for a month, plan it for a month, slowly get the pieces together... and three to four months later, they pull the trigger.

They get there. But the fast-risers get the work done in a quarter of the time. Why?

The answer is FOCUS. None of them have a focusing superpower or cognitive training or even a meditation practice.

But ALL of them have good habits: they set aside time to build their business every day, usually first thing in the morning. In short, they have built themselves a GOLDEN HOUR.

They've practiced the Golden Hour habit long enough for it to become a skill—they might not even recognize it as a skill, because they've been doing it so long that it's just part of them. In fact, many of the fast-growers are surprised that most people DON'T have this skill of focus.

One common thing entrepreneurs tell me is "I think I have ADHD." That's SO common. But what most have is really just a lack of focus.

They get the same work, same tools, same tactics, even the same mentors—but it takes them four times as long to do the work because they don't have a Golden Hour planned into their day.

These same people often haven't missed a workout in five or 10 YEARS. So they CAN do it—they just need someone to tell them to do so.

Fix the Owner, Fix the Business

Here's a tip: if you think you might have ADHD, but you don't have trouble getting your workouts in...you probably don't have ADHD. You probably just don't have focus.

Focus is a skill. You have to practice it to get it, and practice it to keep it.

The good news is that skills can be learned.

One of our insider mantras at Two-Brain is "Fix the owner, Fix the Business." Our mentors understand that if we help the business owner develop the right skills, we will help the business get better results.

More and more, our data set shows that clients with the ability to focus outperform everyone else, even when they're given the SAME strategies and tactics as everyone else.

If you have the skill of focus, you can find the most important work and repeat it over and over, building your business.

Here's one more place FOCUS comes in. Lack of focus makes it hard to get started on the work that matters. But lack of focus also makes it easy to STOP doing the work that matters.

Many gym owners have the motivation to start things. "Make a Facebook post? Got it!" But many also don't have the focus to keep doing what they've learned after the first time.

It's not hard to get someone started on their exercise program. It's very hard to keep them from stopping. Right? Well, it's the same with improving your business. It's not hard for a mentor to get you excited about a new idea. But it's hard for anyone to keep you excited about business tasks.

Another of the key traits of our top-performing gyms is this: when a mentor tells them to do something, they do it and keep doing it until the mentor tells them to stop.

They don't stop writing blog posts when they get bored.

They don't stop running ads when their cost per lead goes up or down.

They don't stop asking for referrals after the first time.

THE GOLDEN HOUR

As John Franklin, the CMO of Two-Brain, likes to say, "Find what works, then keep doing it until it stops working."

Sometimes, gym owners start something and stop before it even has a chance to start working! Sometimes they quit because it's hard; sometimes they quit because they're bored.

In fact, people who are quick to point out a lack of 'discipline' in their gym clients are guilty of the same problem in their business. It's not laziness or ADHD; it's lack of skill. Skill comes from habit, and habits come from practice.

I'll talk more about focus later but let's jump right in to talking about how you can implement the Golden Hour in your business immediately.

DESIGNING THE GOLDEN HOUR

When thinking of how to apply the Golden Hour in your business, it's useful to see it through your eyes as a fitness coach.

Many of us refer to our clients and members as "athletes." We do that to help change their mindset.

We know that if they think of themselves as athletes, they will do what athletes do:

- They will get up on time.
- They will plan their meals in advance.
- They will show up for their workouts and practice their movements.

In short, they will take their fitness seriously.

This doesn't mean that all of our clients will compete in sport or CrossFit or bodybuilding. But you don't have to be competitive to be an athlete; you simply have to be committed to the pursuit of a worthy goal.

Just imagine that you designed a program like this and someone followed it every day:

- Go to the gym.
- Open with warm up exercises.
- Lead with the reps—core exercises you do every day.
- Devote time to a specific weakness given by your coach.
- End after one hour.
- Next step—plan your meals for the day.

That would be a "Golden" start to the day for any "athlete," whatever their goals.

You and I know, as fitness coaches, that if every client spent one hour every day dedicated to improving their health and fitness and kept working out and eating well forever without backsliding, they'd be among the fittest people on the planet.

But we also know, as fitness coaches, that most people spend zero time every day on their health and fitness. Sure, most of our clients are more committed. They spend three or four hours on it per week but even they often skip important stuff like eating well.

Most people don't stick with exercise or nutrition long enough to make a difference. They might try a diet for a couple of weeks, or sign up at your gym and quit after a few months. We know that doesn't produce life-changing health.

The key is not what you do for one day or for one week. It is what you do repeatedly.

The key is PRACTICE.

Practice means getting good repetitions. Practice means building a habit, and building a habit means building a skill.

Practice does not mean constantly changing sports: practice means getting better at your current sport.

It means maintaining your focus. It means repetition, not replacement. It means pursuing the important, not the new.

Maintaining that focus and practice over an extended period of time (with the right coaching) will ensure that anyone reaches their fitness goals.

Mental Athletes

The secret of success in business is exactly the same. That's why I like to say that we, as entrepreneurs, are "mental athletes."

The success of our business lies largely between our ears.

That means we must train our brains the way we train our bodies. Just as we train ourselves for strength; for endurance; for stamina… we must train our memory, our logic and our focus.

Just as we don't get strong by accident, we don't become more focused by accident.

Just as no one is born with amazing endurance, none of us are born with amazing logical thought.

And just as no one does a beautiful power clean on their first attempt, none of us makes the perfect Instagram post on their first try.

The key to growing our business is practice: getting better at the most important things instead of constantly trying to find the fun thing, the easy thing or the new thing.

Again, the key is what we do every day rather than what we do on any one day.

The vital factor about the Golden Hour is that it forces us to create the HABITS and develop the SKILLS that will determine our success.

We'll fill in the details later but here is how the Golden Hour is structured:

- **G**o to a Place Where You Can Focus: Set yourself up for success by doing this somewhere you won't be disturbed.
- **O**pen Your Mind: Get in the right place mentally to make best use of the time.
- **L**ead with Marketing "Reps": Make time for the essential repeated tasks that will get you more clients.
- **D**o Your Big Projects: Set aside time for actions that have a longer term benefit.
- **E**nd After One Hour: Use the time well and be disciplined.
- **N**ext Steps: Plan the rest of your day with checklists.

In the next segment, I'll go through each of the GOLDEN Hour elements in more detail. I'll give you sample marketing actions that you can first implement right away; and then repeat forever.

As you follow through the actions in this book, that is your first 'lap' of the process. You'll get results by following specific directions. To really master any of these skills, though, you'll need objective feedback from a mentor, just as an athlete needs the feedback of their coach to improve their squat.

Before we go into each of the elements, I want to talk about why the timing of when you do the Golden Hour is so important.

THE GOLDEN HOUR SECRET: NEVER COACH THE MORNING CLASS

One of the first—and most important—instructions I got from my mentor was to buy myself an hour of time as cheaply as possible: to hire a cleaner and use that time to work on marketing.

I already understood what the phrase "Working ON your business instead of IN your business" meant: that I should be doing tasks that grew my business instead of doing the everyday tasks required to operate. The problem was that I had no time or money (or so I thought).

I was skeptical about my mentor's instruction, but it worked.

I hired my first cleaner (Shawn) for $14 per hour, three nights every week. While Shawn mopped and vacuumed, I'd sit at the front desk in the gym and do marketing work.

The first night, I sent an email to all of my clients inviting them to purchase a 20-pack of personal training sessions. There was no discount for purchasing large packages, but I sold a 10-pack for $395 right away. By the next morning, I'd already seen a massive ROI on buying back my time.

One problem, though: Shawn cleaned at night. He would show up when the gym closed at 9pm, and I'd sit there and work while he did. But at 9pm, I'd already been at the gym for 15-16 hours. I was exhausted. I was definitely not doing my best work.

I was starting to fix my business, but I was still exhausted and close to burnout. The mentorship was working, but I wasn't sure I could survive long enough to make all of the changes required to save my gym.

My mentor's next suggestion was to replace myself in the morning classes. This would do three things:

1. Allow me to sleep in for at least a half hour (until the late hour of 5am).
2. Buy me an hour of time when my mind was fresh and focused.
3. Allow me to leave the gym when Shawn showed up at 9pm instead of when he finished at 10pm.

The problem was that I didn't trust other people to run the morning classes. They were tiny—only two or three people in them—and didn't generate enough revenue to pay someone else. At that time, someone on my 'unlimited' package was paying about $5 per class if they showed up every day ($135/month, and the 'unlimited' people came EVERY day.)

None of my other coaches would work for minimum wage, and paying someone $20 to coach the class would mean that I was losing money on each class.

But I took his suggestion on a trial basis, and hired the cheapest coach I could find: a sophomore from a local college who was a member at the gym.

Her name was Charity. She didn't have my degrees or certifications yet, but she DID have a big, bright smile at 6am.

She had a lot of energy. She gave huge welcomes to people that I couldn't have shared on my best day. And she did it EVERY day.

People absolutely loved Charity, and the 6am class started to grow. I watched from the corner, sitting at the desk and doing my work.

This is when the business really started to gain momentum. I showed up at 6am to see a group already in session. I sat down and cleared my head by writing 750 words (usually a daily blog post that started with the Workout of the Day.)

Then I got to work on the larger projects that actually saved the gym: writing a staff playbook, marketing to my list, checking in on clients.

I published everything on my blog DontBuyAds, because I didn't want to forget it—and that blog became popular with other gym owners. All of the DontBuyAds posts were written at 6am while Charity coached a few feet away.

This is how my Golden Hour was born: every day at 6am, I sipped coffee and did work that grew my business.

I also got far more focused for the rest of the day. My clients noticed that my mood was much better; I wasn't distracted during every conversation. My client headcount grew for the first time, because of the marketing work I was doing. And my retention went up, too: people loved reading the blog posts, loved knowing more about the science and the "why" behind the workouts.

My staff noticed a big improvement and their attitudes changed too. They started to trust my leadership more and bought into the gym's direction.

After a year of consistent Golden Hour time, my gym had outgrown its space. That growth came from focus—not from reading more audiobooks, not from getting a new marketing idea, not from browsing Facebook (which didn't even really exist yet. Nor did podcasts.) But from setting aside the time to do the work. Actually getting it done.

I was confident in expanding because I knew WHY my gym was growing, and I was confident that it would continue to grow.

Many gym owners start small (smart) and then expand... and it hurts their business. This is because they don't really know what made their business grow in the first place: are they good at business, or was the market just good? Were they capitalizing on the early adopters in their town? Were they just lucky?

But I knew I had a winning combination, and, given enough time, it would keep working. That combination was really focus and mentorship: I knew exactly what to do, and set aside time to do it.

As I said at the start of this book, my rule for over a decade has been: *"Every day, do one thing to grow your business before you do anything else."*

This is how I fixed my gym, started and sold other companies, and grew a blog into the largest mentorship practice in the world for gym owners.

Never by taking one particular step, or having one new idea. ALWAYS by spending 40—60 minutes working on my business before I did anything else that day.

Our largest problem, as entrepreneurs, isn't a lack of good ideas. It's a lack of focus. We jump from one thing to the next thing, and that makes us good at neither.

There's a reason I want you to set up your Golden Hour first thing in the morning.

I know, I know: you're not a 'morning person'. You CAN do it later, but it won't be as effective. This is because, in the morning, your attention is unencumbered. You have not yet become distracted by your email, your social media, the needs of your family, or a ringing phone. So, your brain is fresh.

So, here's your first ACTION STEP: Decide when you will do your Golden Hour each day and schedule it in your diary now.

Now let's talk about exactly what you do in that hour.

G O TO A PLACE WHERE YOU CAN FOCUS
O PEN YOUR MIND
L EAD WITH MARKETING "REPS"
D O YOUR BIG PROJECTS
E ND AFTER ONE HOUR
N EXT STEPS

G

GO TO A PLACE WHERE YOU CAN FOCUS

My daily Golden Hour sessions delivered positive results right from the start. But I wanted to keep getting better results.

With Charity coaching at 6am, I was focusing far better. However, a CrossFit gym is noisy, and I always wanted to watch what was going on. This was distracting for the coach, too—who wants their boss watching their every move?

I knew what I needed was an office with a door that closed. I knew that, undisturbed, I could get even more out of my Golden Hour.

So, my top priority for growing the gym space wasn't to store more barbells or hold larger classes. My #1 "must-have" was an office where I could do my Golden Hour work, because that's what drove the gym forward.

Moving into an office space added gasoline to the fire. I started producing our new OnRamp program, which boosted ARM (client value) and LEG (length of client engagement) and gave the coaches more work. I started measuring our metrics, which gave me a REAL look at what was actually working in my business, and what wasn't.

Then I got to work fixing the stuff that didn't work. I got rid of punch cards. I got rid of Open Gym. I kept up the email marketing. When Facebook arrived, I learned how to use it. And I was able to maximize the value of every audiobook, every course I took because of my Golden Hour.

My gym went from under $10,000 per month to over $70,000 per month during this period. Several of my staff became full time. I started setting profits aside and looking for a building to buy. Again, it wasn't because I learned something different: it was because of FOCUS. I actually did the work.

I'll pause for a minute here: most people reading this book are also reading other books, listening to podcasts, learning about business. You're probably learning faster than I did. You might know more than I did back then.

Some of you probably have a mentor—you might even be in my program. But what you KNOW is less important than what you DO. I am telling this whole story to illustrate that point.

You can't trade your knowledge for rent. You have to act on it.

You want single-minded focus on one task at a time. Later on, I'll talk about the myth of "multitasking" and the problem of context-switching.

The truth is your brain can only focus on one thing at a time, not two, and definitely not three. Switching rapidly between tasks wears you out, erodes your focus and kills your attention.

This is why creating a distraction-free environment for a focused one-hour window each morning is vital.

By doing so, you can harness the full power of your cognitive abilities, ensuring that you give your most important tasks undivided attention. That is essential to maximize productivity and foster business growth.

To create this kind of attention, you have to be intentional about protecting your focus.

That's why it's essential to find a place to do your Golden Hour where people can't disturb you.

Turn off your phone notifications and silence your social media. Resist the urge to check email, click on your notifications, or respond to anyone else.

Set up a timer. My friend Jason Khalipa calls this the "AMRAP mentality": he believes that giving yourself a time limit will force you to work quickly without distractions.

If you have a time limit to complete As Many Reps as Possible (AMRAP), you'll get more done—and it will feel like a game.

Of course, there will be some days when you are not at your best. If you ate poorly or slept badly the evening before, you're going to feel hungover.

But the development of the habit is more important than the quality of your output on any particular day. In other words, get up on time and get to work even when you don't feel like it. Put the Golden Hour right into your calendar.

As my mentor Carrie Wilkerson taught me, "If it's important, it deserves an appointment."

0

OPEN YOUR MIND

TIME REQUIRED: 5-10 MINUTES

To achieve the best results from your Golden Hour, you need to get into the right place mentally as well as being in the right physical location.

Getting there requires you to take specific steps and not just hope for the best.

One good way to do this is to practice a bit of meditation first. If you're good at meditation already, you can sit silently with your eyes closed. But if you're not, this practice will just make you tired. What I recommend is using a journal or a web app like 750words.com to clear the junk out of your mind.

Just write what you're thinking about—the things that worry you, the stuff you are ruminating on (personal or business or anything else), the stuff you're trying hard not to forget. Make lists, rant, or do anything in between. Your job is to get everything out of your head, for now. You'll decide what to let back into your head later.

This is a practice used by writers for centuries called "morning pages". But it's really focused meditation. Get your junk out of your head and onto paper. Don't correct spelling mistakes or grammar or anything else.

You don't have to do the full 750 words—it will be hard at first. Expect it to be hard. Just keep writing for 15 minutes—even write about how much you hate writing. Keep your hand moving and your brain will start to open up.

You're really trying to warm yourself up for the work ahead. This written meditation should feel like a warmup for the work to be done, just as you would do a warmup before hard physical exercise.

If you're a coffee drinker, absolutely keep a warm cup by your side. If not, I recommend keeping a glass of water nearby.

Whichever approach works best for you, just spend 10 minutes getting everything out of your head that's distracting you right now.

L

LEAD WITH MARKETING "REPS"

TIME REQUIRED: 10-15 MINUTES

We start the day with marketing-related tasks. That's because marketing is what grows your business.

Most of our marketing work is having conversations with current clients, former clients and future clients. We'll get into the specifics later.

As our mantra is *"Every day, do one thing to grow your business before you do anything else,"* we make this the priority.

In the next section, I'm going to give you some marketing tasks that work. You'll do them once, and then repeat them, in our six-week Golden Hour challenge. The first reps you perform will take lots of time and might even be a bit frustrating. But they'll get easier every time you do them—15 minutes will be more than enough time eventually.

The key to marketing is momentum. It is like the story of Sisyphus: you have to keep pushing the big rock up the hill every day; if you take one day off, it rolls back down again.

That's why we schedule this segment every day.

We identify what works and we REPEAT it CONSISTENTLY week after week.

We typically suggest identifying one specific marketing task and doing it the same day every week. This is the schedule I'll share with you later in the book:

- **Monday:** Write one blog post or record one Quickcast.
- **Tuesday:** Distribute Monday's content to your email list and social media.
- **Wednesday:** Check in with five clients.
- Thursday: Mine your leads.
- **Friday:** Set up your social media for the following week.
- **Saturday:** Take 10 client pictures or record two video interviews.
- **Sunday:** Send a "weekly preview" message to your staff.

This is the stuff that really builds momentum. Spend 15 minutes on these Marketing "Reps" (repeated tasks) each day. If the tasks take a bit longer, that's okay—you'll get faster as you improve your skill at each. Don't worry, I'll tell you exactly how to do each one shortly.

Marketing is what grows your business. So, if all you can manage, on a given day, is to keep up your marketing habit, your business will keep growing. When the marketing stops, your business slowly coasts to a stop...and then begins to roll backward as clients leave and you don't replace them.

D

DO YOUR BIG PROJECTS

TIME REQUIRED: 30 MINUTES

The largest chunk of your Golden Hour time is daily project work. Projects are longer term initiatives that will take you a few days or even a few weeks. These are usually assigned by your mentor, but some are laid out in my previous book, Gym Owners' Handbook.

Projects are actions that have a positive long-term impact on your business.

The key to remember is that even though the basic marketing work is done now, you're still working ON your business instead of IN your business.

That's an important phrase that helps me remember that answering the phone, sweeping the floor or watching videos about coaching cues doesn't actually grow my business. It just makes me better at the various jobs in my gym—administration, cleaner, and coach.

The Golden Hour is where you do your CEO work. Don't get caught up in other jobs during your CEO time.

In the next segment, we have given you a daily project for the first week of your six-week Golden Hour challenge. These first projects will become your daily marketing work as you get better and faster at them.

Your first priority is to complete all of these steps. Stay focused on these until you complete them.

When you have these marketing tasks down, and completing them has become a habit, the next step is to do the important projects required to grow your business. If you're familiar with the Eisenhower matrix, these are usually the things that fall into the "Important, Not Urgent" sector.

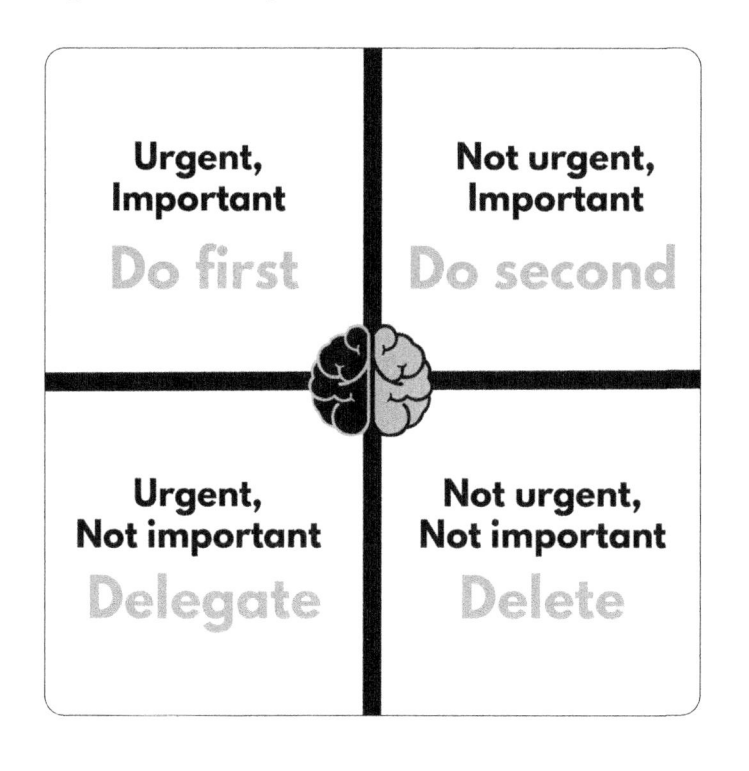

Urgent, Important	Not urgent, Important
Do first	Do second
Urgent, Not important	**Not urgent, Not important**
Delegate	Delete

These projects usually take multiple days and several steps. For example, writing a staff playbook will take a few days and require absolute focus. You'll be tempted to check email or Facebook messages while you're doing it. But your business can't grow until you've established this baseline, because your business will always fall to the level of your systems in tough times and grow to the level of your marketing in good times. A staff playbook is the document that gives your systems life—but it's not fun to write. It's important enough to do it, but lacks the 'urgency' that an Instagram notification sends to your brain.

The larger projects are important, but the real point at this stage is to establish the habit of DOING. Don't get frustrated if your big projects take awhile or don't turn out perfect the first time.

Remember, the purpose of this book is to build the skills that are the foundation for progress.

Many people study ideas, strategies and tactics just to 'collect' knowledge. But as Naval Ravikant said, "If knowledge solved the problem, we'd all be billionaires with six-pack abs." Practice DOING the work.

E

END AFTER ONE HOUR

This is really important. Work for the full hour, but no more. On some occasions, if you happen to be "in flow" and you have time available, you can keep going.

However, if you do extra, you don't get to accumulate extra time and end early tomorrow. You don't get credit for "rollover minutes" when you're building a habit.

In general, create the discipline of working uninterrupted for an hour.

It helps to set a clock and place it out of sight, and then keep working until the buzzer.

If you don't have an hour, here's the key...

Maintaining the habit is more important than executing perfectly every day.

So, if you find yourself short on time on a given day, do the marketing "Reps". They should take about 15 minutes. Then strive to do the full hour the next day. Keeping up the habit matters more than the specific task or project done on any particular day.

Projects really move your business forward, and the marketing tasks maintain what you have. If you can't do the projects because of time, at least do the marketing "Reps" so you don't slip backward.

If you don't have 15 minutes, at the very minimum, keep up your momentum.

Get started early and go to a room with a door that closes.
Open your mind with some written meditation.
Even if you just put five minutes into this, you'll build the habit of waking up on time and starting something.

The first two parts of the GOLDEN acronym are GO for a reason. They're how you start establishing the habits that build the skills that build your business.

The way you finish your session will also give you a running start on the next day. It's actually best to leave a few things undone; to feel as if you have a running start for the next day.

Ernest Hemingway used to end his daily writing time in the middle of a sentence, so that the next day he knew exactly where to start. And once he started, he found it easier to keep going.

The larger point, for us, is to see momentum building. The most important thing is to build the habit—not to do any specific task over another. The key is that habits build skills, and skills build businesses. Even if you only have five minutes, do something to grow your business every day.

N

NEXT STEPS

TIME REQUIRED: 5 MINUTES

The key to maintaining successful momentum is finishing your hour by making your to-do list for the rest of your day.

This will help you get even more done through the day.

But most importantly, you can look back at your list of completed work at the end of the day.

As you complete the work on your list, check it off. You can use whatever approach you like best for keeping track, such as:

- Pen and paper
- Specific apps like Winstreak
- Basic tools like Google Tasks

At the end of the day, you can take a quick glance at your "Done" list and see what you've accomplished.

This is important for building momentum, because while your "to-do" list will never be done forever, it CAN be done for the day.

44 THE GOLDEN HOUR

When you're building skills, just getting the work done is a win, because it builds momentum.

You don't get motivated and then start winning; you start winning and then you get motivated.

Habits get you started on building skills; little wins make the habits easier over time.

THE SIX-WEEK GOLDEN HOUR CHALLENGE

As with anything in life, the most important step toward success with the Golden Hour is starting to put it into practice and making it a consistent part of your day.

However, the Golden Hour is not something you can just switch on and have it running smoothly right away. Not least because there are some procedures and systems that you need to put in place to make it work.

The best way to get started with the Golden Hour is to focus for the first few weeks on setting up the systems you'll need to make it flow smoothly later. As well as putting the systems in place, this will help you hone the skills necessary to ensure success.

To help you do that quickly and easily, I've designed a "Six-Week Golden Hour Challenge" and we'll go through that step by step here.

Remember the Golden Hour is structured as follows:

> **G** O TO A PLACE WHERE YOU CAN FOCUS
> **O** PEN YOUR MIND
> **L** EAD WITH MARKETING "REPS"
> **D** O YOUR BIG PROJECTS
> **E** ND AFTER ONE HOUR
> **N** EXT STEPS

Before you start the 6-Week Golden Hour challenge, you can prepare by choosing a place to do your Golden Hour work; choosing a form of meditation that works for you; setting up a timing device like a stopwatch; and choosing a way to make your "to-do" lists.

Making these decisions in advance will help you begin your Golden Hour practice smoother. Then we'll ease into the process with HABIT STACKING to allow us to get started and then to add more tasks and habits gradually. I'll talk more about that later.

During the Six-Week Challenge, the 'projects' will involve setting up the marketing tasks or "Reps" that you will do every day. Although these activities will eventually take 15 minutes out of your day, it will take longer to set them up at the start.

As with any skill, your first time through will take you longer. You'll need to set up your accounts; you'll overthink some of the tasks; you'll need to find cut-and-paste samples; etc.

That's okay! Skill acquisition gets faster as you move through the process.

Consider the Six-Week Challenge to be your first "Rep" of these short tasks. These will then become the 15-minute tasks that you

The Six-Week Golden Hour Challenge

start each day with in the future. For now, these are the Projects on which you'll spend your Golden Hour during the first six weeks.

Your weekly schedule of marketing "Reps" will look something like this:

- **Monday:** Write one blog post or record one Quickcast.
- **Tuesday:** Distribute Monday's content to your email list and social media.
- **Wednesday:** Check in with five clients.
- **Thursday:** Mine your leads.
- **Friday:** Set up your social media for the following week.
- **Saturday:** Take 10 client pictures or record two video interviews.
- **Sunday:** Send a "weekly preview" message to your staff.

You may want to play around with this a little bit to suit the way you work best. For example, you might decide that it's better to set up your social media on a Monday than a Friday. But the above example is the best way to get started. Don't let overthinking paralyze you.

To allow for Habit Stacking, we will develop the process as follows:

- **Week 1:** Do the Monday and Tuesday work.
- **Week 2:** Add the Wednesday and Thursday work.
- **Week 3:** Add the Friday work.
- **Week 4:** Add the Saturday work.
- **Week 5:** Add the Sunday work.
- **Week 6:** Complete a full week.

In week one for example, it doesn't mean you only do a Golden Hour on two days. You'll find that it will take more than a day, your first time around, to complete all the elements. It's vital that you allocate time every day and keep up the momentum.

The next few pages provide a step-by-step guide to what you should do each week of the Six-Week Challenge to get this started.

MOMENTUM TRACKER

As you work through your Six-Week Challenge, make sure you track your momentum by marking off each day that you complete your Golden Hour.

PRINTABLE CHECKLIST: DEVELOP YOUR HABITS!

CHECK THE BOXES!

Monday	Tuesday	Wednesday	Thursday	Friday	Saturday	Sunday
☐	☐	☐	☐	☐	☐	☐
☐	☐	☐	☐	☐	☐	☐
☐	☐	☐	☐	☐	☐	☐
☐	☐	☐	☐	☐	☐	☐
☐	☐	☐	☐	☐	☐	☐
☐	☐	☐	☐	☐	☐	☐

Every day, do one thing to grow your business before you do anything else!

Two-Brain Business

Watch the demos at
www.goldenhourchallenge.com

THE SIX-WEEK GOLDEN HOUR CHALLENGE
Weekly Instructions

CHALLENGE WEEK ONE: SET UP CONTENT CREATION AND DISTRIBUTION

Your first two days of the week will be as follows:

- **Monday:** Write one blog post or record one Quickcast.
- **Tuesday:** Distribute Monday's content to your email list and social media.

However, setting these up takes a bit of time and each step will take you longer the first time around. Hence, I suggest that for your first week, you focus only on these two elements.

Monday: Content Creation

The aim of this step is to set up the systems needed to complete the Monday marketing task of writing one blog post or recording one QuickCast.

Our long-term goal here is to create the marketing content to support building your brand and attracting new clients.

When you create content through your blog or QuickCast, you will use it over and over again. It will boost your other marketing funnels by warming your audience up. We teach gym owners to build four funnels for marketing: referral, social, paid ads and content. The different funnels work together, and are more than the sum of their parts. Your content boosts all of the rest and improves retention, too. It's never been more important to publish content consistently. Luckily, it's also never been easier.

Your blog or QuickCast will be shared on your social media channels. And your social media channels exist to pull people to your website... where you can move them down the marketing funnel toward a No-Sweat Intro.

Of the four marketing funnels every gym needs, two are media-based (the content funnel and the social media funnel). And the third (your paid ads funnel) works many times better if you have a consistent content funnel and a social media funnel.

Think about how you found Two-Brain Business, or even this book: you might have seen an ad or a social media post, or found the podcast; then you consumed more content, and tried some of it in your gym.

Only after we'd built a relationship did you make a purchase. 95% of the content I make is free; 5% is a real investment (mentorship, my actual service). This is the new internet economy: you need to give knowledge away for free, and charge for your valuable service.

Blog or QuickCast?

First question: what's easiest for you—to write, or to record your voice?

That question alone should help you decide whether to blog or to QuickCast.

A blog is a 250-500 word informational post. I built Catalyst, Ignitegym, and Two-Brain Business with a blog, and it's still the most trusted source of information.

A QuickCast is a 5-10 minute informational podcast. You're going to talk about the same topics, but some people prefer to talk instead of to write. No problem.

Overcoming the Big Roadblock

I'll give you a topic in a moment. But first: the big roadblock.

Why don't more people publish more often? There are many excuses, but only one real reason: the Resistance.

The Resistance is an imaginary force that stops you from publishing. It says "I'm not good enough", or "I'm not ready" or "Nobody wants to hear from me" or "People will think I have a big ego!" Or, most often, "I don't have permission!"

None of these are true—the Resistance lies.

We imagine that publishing our thoughts will hurt our reputation or our "brand"—both of which are also imaginary.

- ▶ You're not going to be a great writer when you publish your first post. Do it anyway.
- ▶ You're not going to feel inspired to record your first QuickCast. Record one anyway.
- ▶ You're never going to have a unique idea that no one else has ever written down. Write it down anyway.

Do it because you want to help people. Do it because it's Monday, and on Monday you publish.

Great content producers aren't born. They screw up a lot and try to get better. Some get pretty good, and their newer stuff buries their older stuff. The key is to keep publishing.

How to Create Good Content

Creating a good blog post or QuickCast is much easier than you probably think. You just need to think about the last question a client asked you—or think about what a relative asked you about fitness over dinner.

Pretend that person is right in front of you. Then type your answer. It's that easy.

New bloggers worry too much about formatting and language—but people relate to conversational, personable language.

My best blog posts always get the response "OMG, are you inside my head?!?" or "Dude—did you write this JUST for me?"

Don't worry about the hooks or the SEO keywords—I never have. Simply putting something out there is enough to build a gym (heck, it's been enough to build an eight-figure business for me and a nine-figure business for giants like CrossFit.)

For now, here's your first topic:

"What made you open a gym in the first place?"

Either write a letter—pretend you're writing it to me—or record a voicemail on your phone.

You then publish your letter as a blog on your website or your voicemail as a QuickCast on your podcast hosting platform.

FOR A STEP-BY-STEP GUIDE ON HOW TO CREATE GOOD CONTENT, SEE APPENDIX 1 OR VIEW THE VIDEO BY TAKING A PICTURE OF THIS QR CODE WITH YOUR PHONE:

Once you have published your first one, you will repeat this every Monday at the start of your Golden Hour.

To recap, your first Monday should look like this:

G—go to a place where you can focus

O—open your mind with some meditation

L—lead with the marketing reps: start setting up and producing a blog post or a QuickCast

D—do your projects: continue setting up and producing your first blog post or Quickcast

E—end at the hour (don't worry, you can finish tomorrow if you need to)

N—next steps: write your to-do list for the day. These should be any of the normal day-to-day operational tasks you normally do.

Tuesday: Content Distribution

The purpose of this step is to set up the process needed to complete the Tuesday marketing task of distributing the content you created on Monday through your main channels such as:

- Your email list
- Instagram
- Facebook page
- Public Facebook group
- Google Business Profile

The goal is to ensure the content you have created reaches the widest audience possible so you build your brand, attract new clients and establish stronger relationships with your existing clients.

You will repeat this every Tuesday.

FOR A STEP-BY-STEP GUIDE ON HOW TO DISTRIBUTE YOUR CONTENT, SEE APPENDIX 2 OR VIEW THE VIDEO BY TAKING A PICTURE OF THIS QR CODE WITH YOUR PHONE:

At the end of week one, you should be almost ready to pick up the routine of doing these tasks every Monday and Tuesday. They should eventually take you about 15 minutes but the schedule for the first six weeks is flexible, allowing you to allocate a bit more time to it over the early weeks.

To recap, your first Tuesday should look like this:

G—go to a place where you can focus

O—open your mind with some meditation

L—lead with the marketing reps: start distributing your first blog post or QuickCast. If you haven't completed Monday's work yet, finish that first.

D—do your projects: distribute your first blog post or QuickCast. If you haven't completed Monday's work yet, finish that first.

E—end at the hour (don't worry, you can finish tomorrow if you need to)

N—next steps: write your to-do list for the day. These should be any of the normal day-to-day operational tasks you normally do.

Wednesday:

- **G**—go to a place where you can focus
- **O**—open your mind with some meditation
- **L**—lead with the marketing reps: work on Monday's task to completion. If you're done, work on Tuesday's task to completion. If that's done, you can skip to Next Steps.
- **D**—do your projects: work on Monday's task to completion. If you're done, work on Tuesday's task to completion. If that's done, you can skip to Next Steps.
- **E**—end at the hour (don't worry, you can finish tomorrow if you need to)
- **N**—next steps: write your to-do list for the day. These should be any of the normal day-to-day operational tasks you normally do.

Thursday:

- **G**—go to a place where you can focus
- **O**—open your mind with some meditation
- **L**—lead with the marketing reps: work on Monday's task to completion. If you're done, work on Tuesday's task to completion. If that's done, you can skip to Next Steps.
- **D**—do your projects: work on Monday's task to completion. If you're done, work on Tuesday's task to completion. If that's done, you can skip to Next Steps.
- **E**—end at the hour (don't worry, you can finish tomorrow if you need to)
- **N**—next steps: write your to-do list for the day. These should be any of the normal day-to-day operational tasks you normally do.

Friday:

G—go to a place where you can focus

O—open your mind with some meditation

L—lead with the marketing reps: work on Monday's task to completion. If you're done, work on Tuesday's task to completion. If that's done, you can skip to Next Steps.

D—do your projects: work on Monday's task to completion. If you're done, work on Tuesday's task to completion. If that's done, you can skip to Next Steps.

E—end at the hour (don't worry, you can finish tomorrow if you need to)

N—next steps: write your to-do list for the day. These should be any of the normal day-to-day operational tasks you normally do.

Saturday:

G—go to a place where you can focus

O—open your mind with some meditation

Sunday:

G—go to a place where you can focus

O—open your mind with some meditation

CHALLENGE WEEK TWO: ADD CLIENT CONNECTION AND MINING LEADS

Once you are up and running with your Golden Hour, your first four days of the week will be as follows:

- **Monday:** Write one blog post or record one Quickcast.
- **Tuesday:** Distribute yesterday's content to your email list and social media.
- **Wednesday:** Check in with five clients.
- **Thursday:** Mine your leads.

However, you are still getting used to the process and setting these up takes a bit of time. It's normal that each step will take you longer the first time around.

As we have focused on the tasks for Monday and Tuesday in the first week of the Challenge, these should now be taking up less of your time. In the second week, we can add the tasks for Wednesday and Thursday...but only when you've repeated the Monday and Tuesday work. Build the habits!

Monday:

G—go to a place where you can focus

O—open your mind with some meditation

L—lead with the marketing reps: Produce a blog post or a QuickCast

D—do your projects: finish producing your blog post or Quickcast

E—end at the hour

N—next steps: write your to-do list for the day. These should be any of the normal day-to-day operational tasks you normally do.

Tuesday:

G—go to a place where you can focus

O—open your mind with some meditation

L—lead with the marketing reps: Distribute your blog post or QuickCast.

D—do your projects: Distribute your blog post or QuickCast from Monday. This should be getting easier and faster.

E—end at the hour

N—next steps: write your to-do list for the day. These should be any of the normal day-to-day operational tasks you normally do.

Wednesday: Check in with five clients

The Wednesday marketing task is checking in with five of your current clients. The goal is to book your clients in for a Goal Review meeting. The secondary benefit is to ensure your clients have regular contact that helps them get better results and strengthens your relationship with them.

Your clients should have regularly-scheduled goal reviews, where you measure their progress and update their exercise and nutrition plan.

But if your clients aren't on a regular schedule yet, you should start by messaging five at a time (or 20 per month) to get them booked in for their first goal review.

Start a private message with five clients. If most of your clients are on Facebook, use Facebook Messenger. Otherwise, use text.

First message: *"Hey [client]! It's [coach] here from [gym]. How's it going?"*

Then follow the text flowchart on the following page.

The Six-Week Golden Hour Challenge

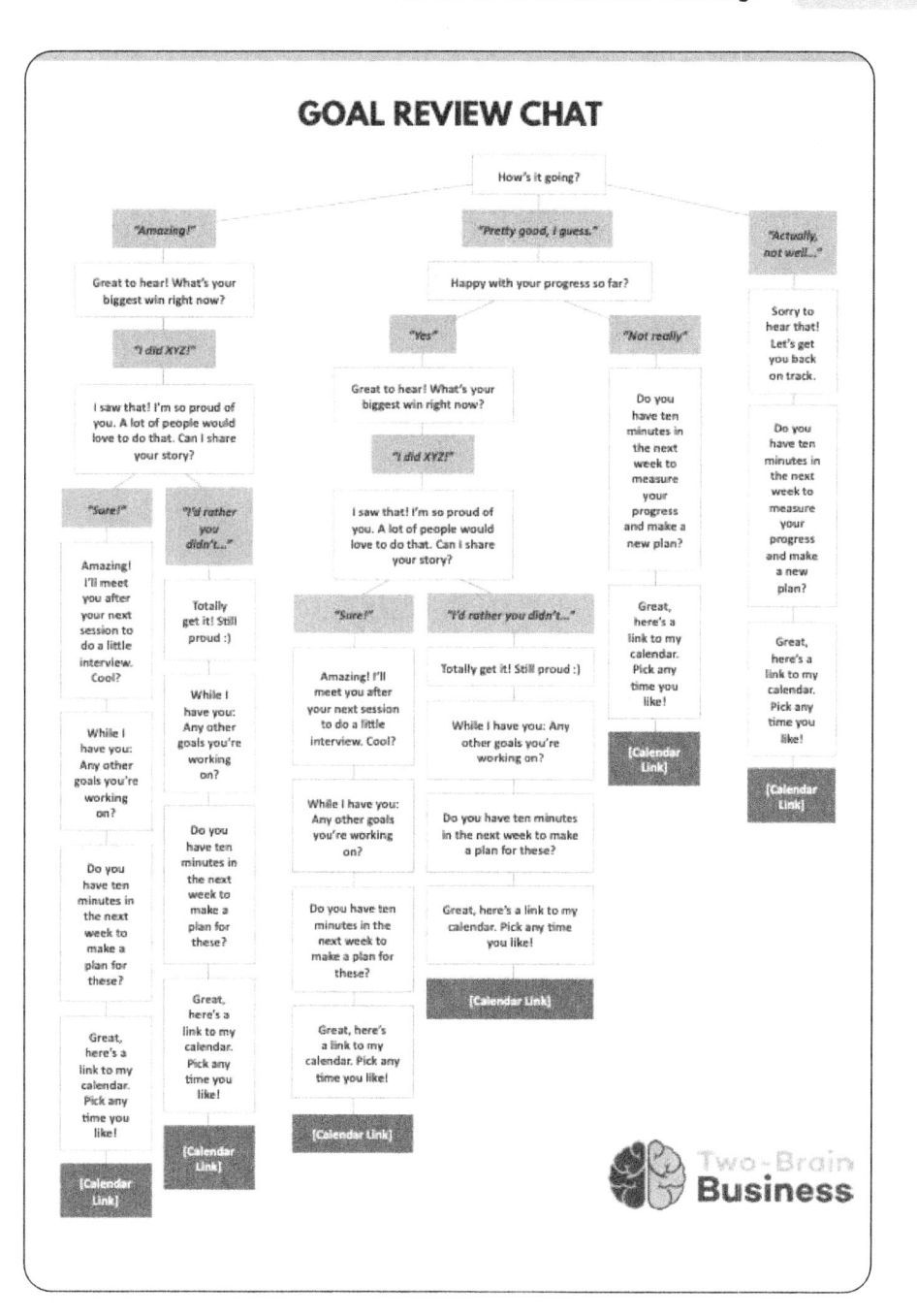

GOAL REVIEW CHAT

How's it going?

"Amazing!"

Great to hear! What's your biggest win right now?

"I did XYZ!"

I saw that! I'm so proud of you. A lot of people would love to do that. Can I share your story?

- **"Sure!"** — Amazing! I'll meet you after your next session to do a little interview. Cool?
  - While I have you: Any other goals you're working on?
  - Do you have ten minutes in the next week to make a plan for these?
  - Great, here's a link to my calendar. Pick any time you like!
  - [Calendar Link]

- **"I'd rather you didn't..."** — Totally get it! Still proud :)
  - While I have you: Any other goals you're working on?
  - Do you have ten minutes in the next week to make a plan for these?
  - Great, here's a link to my calendar. Pick any time you like!
  - [Calendar Link]

"Pretty good, I guess."

Happy with your progress so far?

"Yes"

Great to hear! What's your biggest win right now?

"I did XYZ!"

I saw that! I'm so proud of you. A lot of people would love to do that. Can I share your story?

- **"Sure!"** — Amazing! I'll meet you after your next session to do a little interview. Cool?
  - While I have you: Any other goals you're working on?
  - Do you have ten minutes in the next week to make a plan for these?
  - Great, here's a link to my calendar. Pick any time you like!
  - [Calendar Link]

- **"I'd rather you didn't..."** — Totally get it! Still proud :)
  - While I have you: Any other goals you're working on?
  - Do you have ten minutes in the next week to make a plan for these?
  - Great, here's a link to my calendar. Pick any time you like!
  - [Calendar Link]

"Not really"

Do you have ten minutes in the next week to measure your progress and make a new plan?

Great, here's a link to my calendar. Pick any time you like!

[Calendar Link]

"Actually, not well..."

Sorry to hear that! Let's get you back on track.

Do you have ten minutes in the next week to measure your progress and make a new plan?

Great, here's a link to my calendar. Pick any time you like!

[Calendar Link]

Two-Brain Business

Your goal is to book five clients in for Goal Reviews.

When you meet with them, you'll follow the Goal Review Script. We provide a verbatim script in our mentorship program, but the basic template is this:

1. Measure the client's progress.
2. Ask, "are you completely satisfied with your progress?"
3. If they say "Yes!" then ask them to share their story.
4. If they say anything else, then upgrade their exercise and nutrition plan.
5. Ask for a referral.
6. Book their next goal review.

Remember to book their next goal review before they leave their first!

FOR A STEP-BY-STEP GUIDE ON HOW TO REACH OUT TO YOUR CLIENTS, SEE APPENDIX 3 OR VIEW THE VIDEO BY TAKING A PICTURE OF THIS QR CODE WITH YOUR PHONE:

To recap, your Wednesday should look like this:

G—go to a place where you can focus

O—open your mind with some meditation

L—lead with the marketing reps: start the client check-in process

D—do your projects: continue the client check-in process

E—end at the hour (don't worry, you can finish on Friday if you need to)

N—next steps: write your to-do list for the day.

Thursday: Mine Your Leads

This week we also want to establish the process for the Thursday marketing task of mining your leads.

Our goal is to create a regular process of reaching out to new potential clients.

The aim here is to reach out consistently to new people who are potentially interested in signing up for your gym.

So, who are the most likely people to sign up?

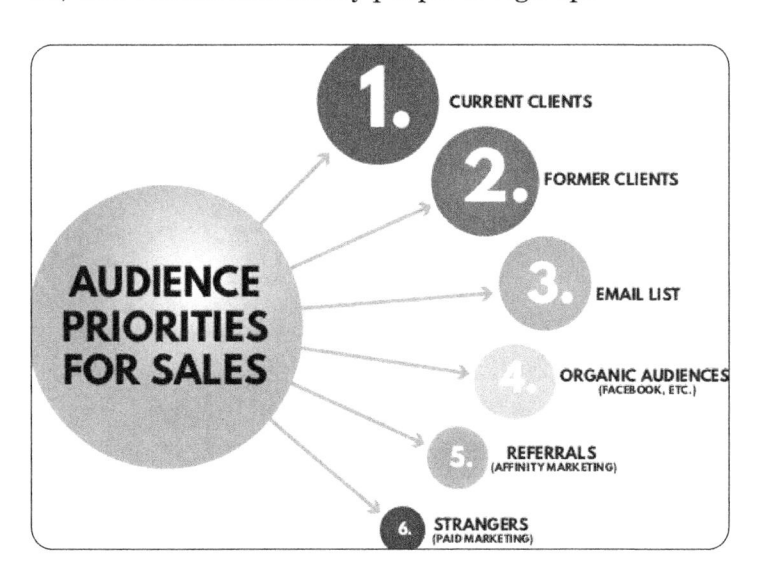

AUDIENCE PRIORITIES FOR SALES

1. CURRENT CLIENTS
2. FORMER CLIENTS
3. EMAIL LIST
4. ORGANIC AUDIENCES (FACEBOOK, ETC.)
5. REFERRALS (AFFINITY MARKETING)
6. STRANGERS (PAID MARKETING)

- First, the people who are already your clients. They're likely to sign up for more.
- Next, the friends and family of your current clients. They've heard all about you.
- Then, your former clients. They already know, like and trust you; they've just taken some time off and fallen out of the habit of using your service.
- Next, the people following your emails or your social media. These people are paying attention; they're just not paying you money yet.
- Finally, strangers—the 'cold leads' who have never heard of you (but might be looking). This is where paid advertising comes in. Paid ads are important, but not part of our daily recurring tasks.

Today, we're going to use Direct Messaging (called a "DM" on Instagram, or "Messenger" on Facebook), text, email, and even the phone to reach out to these people.

We're going to go mining for leads in four ways:

1. DM five Instagram followers
2. Email five former clients
3. Initiate "Sell by Chat" with five clients on Facebook
4. Text five leads who didn't convert

FOR A STEP-BY-STEP GUIDE ON HOW TO MINE YOUR LEADS, SEE APPENDIX 4 OR VIEW THE VIDEO BY TAKING A PICTURE OF THIS QR CODE WITH YOUR PHONE:

The Six-Week Golden Hour Challenge

To recap, your Thursday should look like this:

G—go to a place where you can focus

O—open your mind with some meditation

L—lead with the marketing reps: start the Mine Your Leads process

D—do your projects: continue the Mine Your Leads process

E—end at the hour (don't worry, you can finish tomorrow if you need to)

N—next steps: write your to-do list for the day.

Friday:

G—go to a place where you can focus

O—open your mind with some meditation

L—lead with the marketing reps: work on Monday's task to completion. If you're done, work on Tuesday's task to completion. If that's done, work on Wednesday's task to completion. If that's done, work on Thursday's task to completion.

D—do your projects: work on Monday's task to completion. If you're done, work on Tuesday's task to completion. If that's done, work on Wednesday's task to completion. If that's done, work on Thursday's task to completion.

E—end at the hour (don't worry, you can finish tomorrow if you need to)

N—next steps: write your to-do list for the day.

Saturday:

- **G**—go to a place where you can focus
- **O**—open your mind with some meditation
- **L**—lead with the marketing reps: work on Monday's task to completion. If you're done, work on Tuesday's task to completion. If that's done, work on Wednesday's task to completion. If that's done, work on Thursday's task to completion. If those are all done, skip to Next Steps.
- **D**—do your projects: work on Monday's task to completion. If you're done, work on Tuesday's task to completion. If that's done, work on Wednesday's task to completion. If that's done, work on Thursday's task to completion. If those are all done, skip to Next Steps.
- **E**—end at the hour (don't worry, you can finish tomorrow if you need to)
- **N**—next steps: write your to-do list for the day.

Sunday:

G—go to a place where you can focus

O—open your mind with some meditation

L—lead with the marketing reps: work on Monday's task to completion. If you're done, work on Tuesday's task to completion. If that's done, work on Wednesday's task to completion. If that's done, work on Thursday's task to completion. If those are all done, skip to Next Steps.

D—do your projects: work on Monday's task to completion. If you're done, work on Tuesday's task to completion. If that's done, work on Wednesday's task to completion. If that's done, work on Thursday's task to completion. If those are all done, skip to Next Steps.

E—end at the hour (don't worry, we'll get faster next week.)

N—next steps: write your to-do list for the day.

CHALLENGE WEEK THREE: PLAN YOUR SOCIAL MEDIA IN ADVANCE

Once you are up and running with your Golden Hour, your weekdays will be as follows:

- **Monday:** Write one blog post or record one Quickcast.
- **Tuesday:** Distribute yesterday's content to your email list and social media.
- **Wednesday:** Check in with five clients.
- **Thursday:** Mine your leads.
- **Friday:** Set up your social media for the following week.

In the first two weeks of the Challenge, we have focused on the tasks for Monday through Thursday. These should now be taking up less of your time but the schedule is currently flexible enough to allow you to take time to get used to the systems and processes.

This week, we can now add the Friday task to the schedule.

Monday:

G—go to a place where you can focus

O—open your mind with some meditation

L—lead with the marketing reps: Produce a blog post or a QuickCast

D—do your projects: finish producing your blog post or Quickcast

E—end at the hour

N—next steps: write your to-do list for the day.

Tuesday:

G—go to a place where you can focus

O—open your mind with some meditation

L—lead with the marketing reps: Distribute your blog post or QuickCast.

D—do your projects: Distribute your blog post or QuickCast from Monday. This should be getting easier and faster.

E—end at the hour

N—next steps: write your to-do list for the day.

Wednesday:

G—go to a place where you can focus

O—open your mind with some meditation

L—lead with the marketing reps: start the client check-in process

D—do your projects: continue the client check-in process

E—end at the hour

N—next steps: write your to-do list for the day.

Thursday:

G—go to a place where you can focus

O—open your mind with some meditation

L—lead with the marketing reps: start the Mine Your Leads process

D—do your projects: continue the Mine Your Leads process

E—end at the hour

N—next steps: write your to-do list for the day.

Friday: Plan Your Social Media for Next Week

The Friday task is to set up your social media for the following week. The aim of this is to create a regular process for ensuring consistent widespread distribution of your media content.

The best way to make your social media posting quick each morning is to plan it in advance.

This plan is called an "editorial calendar" and we provide one to every client in Two-Brain Business as a spreadsheet. There's a sample below.

On the calendar, there's a row for each day, and a column for each type of media planned (one column for a picture, one for a caption, and one for a call to action.)

Then you also have a column with check-boxes for each platform you use: one for Instagram, one for Facebook, and one for Google Business Profiles, for example.

While the platforms will change in the future, your media will not; and making the same post on all platforms will save you a lot of time.

The editorial calendar should also have your common hashtags listed for easy copy-and-pasting, and a link to your No-Sweat Intro too.

Here is a week's worth of themes to get you started:

- **Monday:** Post a picture of a smiling client with a testimonial about their progress. Call to action: Book a No-Sweat Intro to get started (link).

- **Tuesday:** Distribute Monday's post on all platforms (Facebook, Instagram, Twitter, LinkedIn). Call to action: read the post or listen to the QuickCast.

- **Wednesday:** Share a short video of a trainer demonstrating a new exercise or workout tip.

- **Thursday:** Post an infographic with nutrition tips or a healthy recipe. Call to action: Book a No-Sweat Intro to get started (link).

- **Friday:** Share a motivational quote with a high-quality image of the gym or a workout session. Call to action: Book a No-Sweat Intro to get started (link).

The Six-Week Golden Hour Challenge 69

- **Saturday:** Highlight a staff member, sharing their role at the gym and a fun fact about them.
- **Sunday:** Share a success story of a member, highlighting their journey and achievements. Call to action: Book a No-Sweat Intro to get started (link).

Your editorial calendar should look like this:

Insert Call to Action Link Here: [Your Link for No-Sweat Intro]

Insert Your Gym's Hashtags Here: [Your Hashtags]

Day	Theme	Caption	Pub Date	URL	Blog	Email	FB	IG	YT
Monday	smiling client picture	-	-	☐	☐	☐	☐	☐
Tuesday	Monday's post	-	-	☐	☐	☐	☐	☐
Wednesday	Exercise demo	-	-	☐	☐	☐	☐	☐
Thursday	infographic	-	-	☐	☐	☐	☐	☐
Friday	motivational quote	-	-	☐	☐	☐	☐	☐
Saturday	staff profile	-	-	☐	☐	☐	☐	☐
Sunday	member profile	-	-	☐	☐	☐	☐	☐

Remember to paste your commonly-used hashtags and a link to your NSI booking in the document for easy cut-and-paste access.

As with creating your blog posts, you can use AI to generate some of these captions for you. For example, you can upload a picture and have ChatGPT find a matching motivational quote. Other software will create the infographics for you, or condense a client story into an attention-grabbing post.

Some CRM software will allow you to build these posts in advance right on the platform, and then auto-post them to your social media platforms for you.

FOR A STEP-BY-STEP GUIDE ON HOW TO PLAN YOUR SOCIAL MEDIA POSTS, SEE APPENDIX 5 OR VIEW THE VIDEO BY TAKING A PICTURE OF THIS QR CODE WITH YOUR PHONE:

To recap, your Friday should look like this:

G—go to a place where you can focus

O—open your mind with some meditation

L—lead with the marketing reps: start planning your Social Media posts for next week.

D—do your projects: continue the Social Media planning process

E—end at the hour (don't worry, you can finish tomorrow if you need to)

N—next steps: write your to-do list for the day.

Saturday:

G—go to a place where you can focus

O—open your mind with some meditation

L—lead with the marketing reps: work on Monday's task to completion. If you're done, work on Tuesday's task to completion. If that's done, work on Wednesday's task to completion. If that's done, work on Thursday's task to completion. If that's done, work on Friday's task to completion. If those are all done, skip to Next Steps.

D—do your projects: work on Monday's task to completion. If you're done, work on Tuesday's task to completion. If that's done, work on Wednesday's task to completion. If that's done, work on Thursday's task to completion. If that's done, work on Friday's task to completion.If those are all done, skip to Next Steps.

E—end at the hour (don't worry, you can finish tomorrow if you need to)

N—next steps: write your to-do list for the day.

Sunday:

- **G**—go to a place where you can focus
- **O**—open your mind with some meditation
- **L**—lead with the marketing reps: work on Monday's task to completion. If you're done, work on Tuesday's task to completion. If that's done, work on Wednesday's task to completion. If that's done, work on Thursday's task to completion. If that's done, work on Friday's task to completion. If those are all done, skip to Next Steps.
- **D**—do your projects: work on Monday's task to completion. If you're done, work on Tuesday's task to completion. If that's done, work on Wednesday's task to completion. If that's done, work on Thursday's task to completion. If that's done, work on Friday's task to completion. If those are all done, skip to Next Steps.
- **E**—end at the hour (don't worry, we'll get faster as we go.)
- **N**—next steps: write your to-do list for the day.

CHALLENGE WEEK FOUR: COLLECT CLIENT TESTIMONIALS

Once you are up and running with your Golden Hour, your first six days of the week will be as follows:

- **Monday:** Write one blog post or record one Quickcast.
- **Tuesday:** Distribute yesterday's content to your email list and social media.
- **Wednesday:** Check in with five clients.
- **Thursday:** Mine your leads.
- **Friday:** Set up your social media for the following week.
- **Saturday:** Take 10 client pictures or record two video interviews.

We are now ready to add the Saturday task to our routine. Here's your week in more detail:

Monday:

G—go to a place where you can focus

O—open your mind with some meditation

L—lead with the marketing reps: Produce a blog post or a QuickCast

D—do your projects: finish producing your blog post or Quickcast

E—end at the hour

N—next steps: write your to-do list for the day. These should be any of the normal day-to-day operational tasks you normally do.

Tuesday:

G—go to a place where you can focus

O—open your mind with some meditation

L—lead with the marketing reps: Distribute your blog post or QuickCast.

D—do your projects: Distribute your blog post or QuickCast from Monday. This should be getting easier and faster.

E—end at the hour

N—next steps: write your to-do list for the day. These should be any of the normal day-to-day operational tasks you normally do.

Wednesday:

G—go to a place where you can focus

O—open your mind with some meditation

L—lead with the marketing reps: start the client check-in process

D—do your projects: continue the client check-in process

E—end at the hour

N—next steps: write your to-do list for the day.

Thursday:

- **G**—go to a place where you can focus
- **O**—open your mind with some meditation
- **L**—lead with the marketing reps: start the Mine Your Leads process
- **D**—do your projects: continue the Mine Your Leads process
- **E**—end at the hour
- **N**—next steps: write your to-do list for the day.

Friday:

- **G**—go to a place where you can focus
- **O**—open your mind with some meditation
- **L**—lead with the marketing reps: start planning your Social Media posts for next week.
- **D**—do your projects: continue the Social Media planning process
- **E**—end at the hour (don't worry, you can finish tomorrow if you need to)
- **N**—next steps: write your to-do list for the day.

Saturday: Collect Client Testimonials

We want to build a process for the Saturday task of taking 10 client pictures or recording two video interviews.

The goal is to collect testimonials and share stories of successful clients to attract new ones.

Saturday is usually a more relaxed day in your gym. With fewer classes on the schedule, and clients who aren't on their usual work week timeline, the environment is less rushed.

Use the opportunity to take pictures. If you run one class on Saturdays, it's probably a larger one. Have your secondary coach take at least 10 pictures of the class in action—and always end the class with a group pic inside or outside of your gym.

You want pictures of smiling faces, not pictures of people collapsed everywhere. Put them in front of your logo. The simple rule is "Happy, not hardcore".

After class has finished, grab one or two clients and say: *"I'm so proud of you! Can I share your story on our social media?"*

When they agree, pull out your phone. Ask them these three questions:

- "What brought you to [your gym] in the first place?"
- "What's your favorite part of [your gym]?"
- "What advice would you give to the person you were a year ago?" (pick a date before they joined.)

These will be three to five minutes long, at most.

Have your staff upload the videos and pictures to a Google Drive folder, or somewhere else where you can use them on your website and on your social media Stories and Reels later.

Tag the person when you post so they can reshare with their friends.

This is not an imposition; most people want to be bragged about; and you have a platform that will make them feel famous.

If they don't want to do the interview, no problem—sometimes one person in 10 will decline. Just move on to the next.

If you can't find a client to interview, pick a staff person.

FOR A STEP-BY-STEP GUIDE ON TELLING CLIENT STORIES, SEE APPENDIX 6 OR VIEW THE VIDEO BY TAKING A PICTURE OF THIS QR CODE WITH YOUR PHONE:

To recap, your Saturday should look like this:

G—go to a place where you can focus

O—open your mind with some meditation

L—When it's time to go to the gym, take 10 client pictures or get 2 testimonials

D—do your projects: take 10 client pictures or get 2 testimonials. Upload them to a place you can use them on social media and blog posts later.

E—end at the hour (don't worry, you can finish tomorrow if you need to)

N—next steps: write your to-do list for the day.

Sunday:

G—go to a place where you can focus

O—open your mind with some meditation

L—lead with the marketing reps: work on Monday's task to completion. If you're done, work on Tuesday's task to completion. If that's done, work on Wednesday's task to completion. If that's done, work on Thursday's task to completion. If that's done, work on Friday's task to completion. If that's done, work on Saturday's task to completion. If those are all done, skip to Next Steps.

D—do your projects: work on Monday's task to completion. If you're done, work on Tuesday's task to completion. If that's done, work on Wednesday's task to completion. If that's done, work on Thursday's task to completion. If that's done, work on Friday's task to completion. If that's done, work on Saturday's task to completion. If those are all done, skip to Next Steps.

E—end at the hour (don't worry, we'll get faster as we go.)

N—next steps: write your to-do list for the day.

CHALLENGE WEEK FIVE: ADD STAFF WEEKLY MESSAGING

Once you are up and running with your Golden Hour, your full week of daily marketing tasks will be as follows:

- **Monday:** Write one blog post or record one Quickcast.
- **Tuesday:** Distribute yesterday's content to your email list and social media.
- **Wednesday:** Check in with five clients.
- **Thursday:** Mine your leads.
- **Friday:** Set up your social media for the following week.
- **Saturday:** Take 10 client pictures or record two video interviews.
- **Sunday:** Send a "weekly preview" message to your staff.

Over the first four weeks of the Challenge, we've gradually added new tasks to our routine. This week, we are ready to add the final one, which is the Sunday task. We are now ready to add the Saturday task to our routine. Here's your week in more detail:

Monday:

G—go to a place where you can focus

O—open your mind with some meditation

L—lead with the marketing reps: Produce a blog post or a QuickCast

D—do your projects: finish producing your blog post or Quickcast

E—end at the hour

N—next steps: write your to-do list for the day.

Tuesday:

G—go to a place where you can focus

O—open your mind with some meditation

L—lead with the marketing reps: Distribute your blog post or QuickCast.

D—do your projects: Distribute your blog post or QuickCast from Monday.

E—end at the hour

N—next steps: write your to-do list for the day.

Wednesday:

G—go to a place where you can focus

O—open your mind with some meditation

L—lead with the marketing reps: start the client check-in process

D—do your projects: continue the client check-in process

E—end at the hour

N—next steps: write your to-do list for the day.

Thursday:

G—go to a place where you can focus

O—open your mind with some meditation

L—lead with the marketing reps: Mine Your Leads

D—do your projects: Mine Your Leads

E—end at the hour

N—next steps: write your to-do list for the day.

Friday:

- **G**—go to a place where you can focus
- **O**—open your mind with some meditation
- **L**—lead with the marketing reps: Plan your Social Media posts for next week.
- **D**—do your projects: Plan your Social Media posts for next week.
- **E**—end at the hour
- **N**—next steps: write your to-do list for the day.

Saturday:

- **G**—go to a place where you can focus
- **O**—open your mind with some meditation
- **L**—When it's time to go to the gym, take 10 client pictures or get 2 testimonials
- **D**—do your projects: take 10 client pictures or get 2 testimonials. Upload them to a place you can use them on social media and blog posts later.
- **E**—end at the hour
- **N**—next steps: write your to-do list for the day.

Sunday: Send a Weekly Preview Message to Your Staff

The Sunday task is sending a "weekly preview" message to staff. The goal of this is to keep your staff motivated and informed about their work and about the gym.

This is "internal marketing," and it's just as important as all of your other marketing. This is what keeps your staff excited about your gym and their place in it.

Just as you have to sell strangers on fitness, and sell your clients on continuing to train with you, you have to sell your staff on the vision and the future.

When staff can't see a future at your gym, they'll quit to start their own, or quit to join the new gym down the street. And if all they hear from you is rules and operating procedures and evaluations, they won't feel as if they're being successful.

These 'weekly preview' messages are either a short post or a private QuickCast.

You can post in a private staff group on Facebook or Slack, or you can send a private voice message to your team (because it's much smaller than your client or public lists).

Here's the format:

1. A lesson you learned this week (ideally from one of them)
2. What's coming next week
3. Why you're excited about next week.

My weekly preview to gym staff would look like this:

- Here's a great tip I learned from Coach Jessica this week. (This makes Jessica feel important and lets staff know you value them.)
- A quick preview of next week's group programming, and the intent of each workout. (This works better than doing long lectures about aerobic vs anaerobic training, and helps them explain the workouts to your clients.)
- Something that's going really well in the gym OR something coming up that clients and staff will love.

Send this early Sunday morning. Keep it short, or it will be 'one more thing' for them to learn and remember. This should make their life easier, not be one more unpaid requirement of their job.

FOR A STEP-BY-STEP GUIDE ON HOW TO SEND A WEEKLY PREVIEW TO YOUR STAFF, SEE APPENDIX 7 OR VIEW THE VIDEO BY TAKING A PICTURE OF THIS QR CODE WITH YOUR PHONE:

To recap, your Sunday should look like this:

G—go to a place where you can focus

O—open your mind with some meditation

L—lead with marketing: record a QuickCast or write a short blog post for your staff

D—do your projects: distribute the QuickCast or blog post to your staff

E—end at the hour

N—next steps: write your to-do list for the day.

CHALLENGE WEEK SIX: RUN A COMPLETE WEEK

You are now ready to run through your full week of daily marketing tasks for the week.

- **Monday:** Write one blog post or record one Quickcast.
- **Tuesday:** Distribute yesterday's content to your email list and social media.
- **Wednesday:** Check in with five clients.
- **Thursday:** Mine your leads.
- **Friday:** Set up your social media for the following week.
- **Saturday:** Take 10 client pictures or record two video interviews.
- **Sunday:** Send a "weekly preview" message to your staff.

After this week, you should have the system running smoothly and will be able to complete each of those tasks in about 15 minutes per day. Your goal this week is to Optimize your process: work hard to become efficient at each of the above tasks, so that you'll have time for new Projects in the future.

WEEKS SEVEN AND ONWARD

For the last six weeks, you've been working on setting up your 15-minute marketing blocks each morning. Your "projects" were developing the systems to do this marketing well, and then optimizing yourself to do this marketing efficiently. These projects are now your "reps", and you'll continue to do them forever.

Once you've established your Golden Hour and can complete your marketing "reps" efficiently, you'll be ready for more projects. If these reps take longer than 15 minutes, don't worry—complete the reps, and then spend the time you have left on your Projects. It's okay if your future Projects take a little longer. It's critical to maintain your marketing momentum even if that only leaves you a few minutes to work on your larger Projects each day.

Ideally, though, you'll eventually be able to complete your marketing reps in about 15 minutes, leaving 30 minutes for Project work each day.

So your week will look like this:

Monday:

G—go to a place where you can focus

O—open your mind with some meditation

L—lead with the marketing reps: Produce a blog post or a QuickCast

D—do your projects: work on a Project assigned by your mentor

E—end at the hour

N—next steps: write your to-do list for the day. These should be any of the normal day-to-day operational tasks you normally do.

Tuesday:

G—go to a place where you can focus

O—open your mind with some meditation

L—lead with the marketing reps: Distribute your blog post or QuickCast.

D—do your projects: work on a Project assigned by your mentor

E—end at the hour

N—next steps: write your to-do list for the day. These should be any of the normal day-to-day operational tasks you normally do.

Wednesday:

G—go to a place where you can focus

O—open your mind with some meditation

L—lead with the marketing reps: do 5 client check-ins

D—do your projects: work on a Project assigned by your mentor

E—end at the hour

N—next steps: write your to-do list for the day.

Thursday:

G—go to a place where you can focus

O—open your mind with some meditation

L—lead with the marketing reps: Mine Your Leads

D—do your projects: work on a Project assigned by your mentor

E—end at the hour =

N—next steps: write your to-do list for the day.

Friday:

G—go to a place where you can focus

O—open your mind with some meditation

L—lead with the marketing reps: plan your Social Media posts for next week.

D—do your projects: work on a Project assigned by your mentor

E—end at the hour

N—next steps: write your to-do list for the day.

Saturday:

G—go to a place where you can focus

O—open your mind with some meditation

L—When it's time to go to the gym, take 10 client pictures or get 2 testimonials

D—do your projects: work on a Project assigned by your mentor

E—end at the hour

N—next steps: write your to-do list for the day.

Sunday:

G—go to a place where you can focus

O—open your mind with some meditation

L—lead with marketing: record a QuickCast or write a blog post and share with your staff

D—do your projects: work on a Project assigned by your mentor

E—end at the hour

N—next steps: write your to-do list for the day.

Which Projects Should You Do Next?

The best source of future projects is having a mentor. As you build your skills, your projects will become larger. That means you'll be taking larger and larger steps toward building your business; it also means that the projects will take longer.

Your mentor will know which projects are big enough to move you forward without being so large that you'll fail to complete them.

Some of the first projects we assign to gym owners are:

Build a financial dashboard to track your metrics

Audit your sales and marketing funnels

Map your client journey

Write a staff playbook

Set up "sweep accounts" for moving money.

We guide you through each of those step-by-step in the Two-Brain Business mentorship process.

If you don't have a mentor yet, you can read about these and other projects in my previous book, Gym Owners' Handbook.

If you're done the basics, my book The Simple Six focuses on the six key metrics that drive your business and how to improve them. It lists specific actions that can form the basis of projects. You can build projects for yourself and your staff with this knowledge.

The projects in the books will help you get started—but they're no replacement for a personalized plan, with coaching and accountability, as you'd get in the Two-Brain Business mentorship practice.

THE FOUR PHASES OF GOLDEN HOUR SUCCESS

When you start with your Golden Hour, it's not going to work perfectly for you right from day one, any more than a new client will move perfectly on the first day in your gym.

Mastering the Golden Hour takes time but the seeds of success are sown from the start.

That's why the most important step is getting started.

There are four key phases that you'll work through, as follows:

1. **Practicing focus**
2. **Creating and stacking habits**
3. **Maintaining momentum**
4. **Turning habits into skills**

As you move through these phases, your Golden Hour will become more and more powerful. I'll talk about each of these phases in more detail and how they will help you improve, so you can recognize your growth as it happens.

PHASE 1

PRACTICING FOCUS

It's easy to be busy all the time but one of the key skills you need in your role as CEO is to be busy doing the right things.

You need to be able to identify what actually makes a business grow, and do those things over and over.

One of the most important aspects of this book is really about enhancing your ability to FOCUS, which is a key entrepreneurial skill.

Focus is like a muscle. You need to PRACTICE it if you want it to grow.

One of the reasons the Golden Hour works so well is that it is all about focus. You give yourself a limited time to complete tasks that have been identified as important and you concentrate on getting them done.

A vital element of the Golden Hour is the daily marketing "Reps": the work that must be repeated, every day, to grow your business.

That's why I suggested in the last chapter that you focus on those for the first six weeks.

If you take these exact tactics and do them once, your gym will grow a little.

If you repeat them over and over, your gym will begin to grow exponentially.

And if, someday, if you delegate them to your staff, your gym will grow without you.

Be warned, though: you must build the habit of repeating the basics before you add more. The Achilles Heel of the entrepreneur is novelty: weaker entrepreneurs replace what's working with what's new.

The reality, as I say often, is that knowledge isn't the entrepreneur's biggest problem. Focus is.

You build the skill of focus by practicing the habits in this book.

Focusing on the right activities creates incremental growth. This is key to the *"Every day, do one thing to grow your business before you do anything else"* mantra.

The Multitasking Myth

The opposite of focused work is "multitasking". Multitasking is a myth. The truth is that your brain can only focus on one thing at a time.

When we think we're "multitasking, we're really asking our brain to jump from one topic to another and back again, over and over. This is called "context switching" by neuroscientists, and it has a huge cost on your output.

Context-switching is a productivity thief. Rather than efficiently managing several tasks, it's like a constant game of catch and release, never truly allowing you to focus and give your best to each task. You might feel busy, but you actually accomplish less—and feel more overwhelmed and stressed.

Picture yourself deep in concentration on a complex task when an email alert sounds or a message notification pops up. Your attention is immediately diverted. While it might seem like just a quick interruption, every switch comes with a cost.

Context-switching leads to the following problems:

- **Decreased productivity:** A study by the American Psychological Association (APA) estimates that task-switching can reduce productivity by as much as 40%. This is primarily due to the time our brains need to refocus.
- **Increased stress levels:** Continual task-switching leads to mental fatigue, increasing stress and negatively affecting overall well-being.
- **Errors and decreased quality of work:** In the rush to manage multiple tasks, errors are likely to creep in, decreasing the quality of work produced.

The Golden Hour aims to help you focus and beat context-switching. It is designed so that you can execute on the things that will build your business.

The structure of the Golden Hour ensures that you're not just scrolling Instagram for 60 minutes to start your day.

That's why I gave you step-by-step instructions for specific marketing "Reps" that grow gyms really fast.

When you have those down, you can start to add new projects into your Golden Hour... but these are done in addition to the marketing basics, not instead of the marketing basics.

You'll create more time for these projects by getting better at the basics, not by replacing the basics with new stuff.

The key is to go step by step, focus on what's important now and keep taking action on it until you are ready to move to the next level.

The Importance of Practice

My gym is succeeding in its mission to change 7,000 lives not because I'm the best at everything, but because I'm really good at one or two things—content and conversations.

I'm good at them because I've been practicing both for 20 years. I wasn't born good at blogging and I was horrible at having conversations even through college.

But I practice both every single day. I know my gym will achieve its mission as long as I maintain my practice.

During that 20 year run, I've seen dozens of gyms come and go. As a newer entrepreneur, I was happy to see them fail, because I had a mindset of scarcity. I thought there were only so many clients to go around, and every client in their gym was one less in mine. That was an immature perspective.

I also chased novelty, because I wanted to "beat" them. When they added a new type of treadmill, I thought I had to do the same. When they started running ads in the newspaper, I felt immense pressure to "be there" with them. This was also an immature mindset.

Over time, I learned that doing the basics really well—offering great coaching; publishing blogs; and having conversations with people—would grow my gym forever, and it didn't matter what anyone else did. Success lay in the pursuit of excellence instead of the pursuit of novelty.

A final note: you might understand now that it's better to get good at one or two things rather than to try and do everything.

Bruce Lee put it this way: *"I fear not the man who has practiced 10,000 kicks once, but I fear the man who has practiced one kick 10,000 times."*

This book will help you get really good at the few things that matter most. But simply repeating a tactic won't make you great.

There's a common myth in education called "the 10,000 hour rule." It states that practicing any skill for 10,000 hours will make you a master.

That's not quite true. The 10,000 hours has to be GOOD practice. That means the practice should be done with a teacher. It means the practice should be challenging. It means that performance should be measured over time.

You can't just walk for 10,000 hours and then win a marathon. You must dedicate yourself to improvement through practice. This is the pursuit of virtuosity—which we'll talk more about later—doing the simple things better and better instead of doing the complicated things once.

And the first step to virtuosity is focus.

PHASE 2

CREATING AND STACKING HABITS

While skills like focus can be learned, doing so takes time and commitment. The key is establishing the right habits first.

We see this when a new gym owner joins the Two-Brain Business mentorship program. Sometimes, a gym is doing really well. Other times, they're in a rough state and anything we give them could be "the thing" they need to start growing again.

But many times, the gym owner doesn't even know how bad their gym is doing. They think "I'm holding about even," but they're really going backward. They just don't see it, because they aren't looking at the right things.

These are smart, caring people who own gyms for all the right reasons. They can work harder than almost any other entrepreneurs I know. But they're usually failing for one of these reasons:

- ► Someone told them that being a better trainer or coach would make them a better business owner.

- They have five training certifications but no knowledge of basic financial accounting.
- They know the top lifts of every client in their gym but don't know if they were profitable last month.
- Their clients love them but won't train with any other coach in the gym.
- They listen to every podcast and read 50 books every year, but don't act on any of it.
- Their staff sticks around for about three years, and then opens their own gym in the same town.
- They're working harder than they were as a coach, but making less money.
- They're underpriced, so they can't afford to pay their staff well—but they do anyway, sacrificing their family's income every week.
- They're running out of time.

I've been guilty of ALL of these. We address all of them in our mentorship program. But we don't tackle all of them at once, because to do so would be to make things worse for the gym owner.

We approach these problems in steps:

- First, we build a high-value onboarding service that will make a real difference in their clients' lives.
- Then we teach them how to present that service properly. The gym owner immediately starts making more money, setting their clients up for success, and keeping their clients longer.
- Next, we start bringing in more clients. We build three separate funnels together, and work step by step through lead generation, lead nurture, and coaching the client to sign up ("selling").

When the gym owner is making more money, we start putting some of these tactics on 'repeat'.

We build the habits that create the long-term skills BEFORE we start layering in the bigger projects. That keeps the new clients coming, the excitement high, and the momentum starts to build.

When the gym owner is consistent with their habits, we add in some medium-sized projects. We standardize their operations, so the business can operate with excellence even when the owner is not there.

Then we add in other levels such as a fourth marketing funnel and a retention strategy and work on upgrading their team.

Put together, these form the operations of the business. The best gyms deliver these operations with excellence. Together, these processes form the foundation of their business.

In short, this is what we aim to do:

- **SYSTEMIZE** everything (including marketing). Put the systems on repeat.
- **OPTIMIZE** everything (including their staff and how they deliver the service).
- **AUTOMATE** what we can, through hiring or other tools.

You can read about many of these systems in my book, Gym Owners Handbook.

Doing all this means the owner increases their income, builds real careers for staff, and scales up the clients they can work with.

Your business doesn't rise to the level of your best idea. It falls to the level of what you repeat over and over again.

As the CEO, you are the ceiling that limits how far your business can rise. Your Standard Operating Procedures are the floor that determine how far you can fall.

You lift your business by systemizing what works and repeating it forever and ever. Your business is what you repeatedly do.

So how does all this fit in with the Golden Hour?

First, you systemize your operations.

Then you repeat them forever (or until they stop working).

But you don't add new ideas, operations, or brainstorms until you've got the basics nailed.

You don't try to add a new social media strategy until you're doing your basic marketing every day, without fail, even when you're bored, even when you're tired, even when you're away. You need to know that the basics get done, no matter what, every single day.

This is a skill. And the skill is built by the habit of focusing on the basics.

New ideas must build on the foundation of solid habits. If new ideas compete with the basics for time, you'll never build a floor to your business, let alone lift it higher. You'll just keep jumping up and falling back down to ground level again.

Habit Stacking

Skills aren't developed overnight; they are built through consistent, habitual practice. It's like fitness—you already know that your clients who just keep showing up, doing the work, and watching their diet will eventually be successful.

It's the same with achieving success in your business.

One effective method to build the skills that build your business is called "habit stacking."

Habit stacking involves starting with a few manageable habits and gradually adding more, establishing a routine that creates growth.

For gym owners, this means doing the small, daily actions that contribute to the overall success of the business.

That's why we have you start out your Golden Hour by adopting the marketing tactics gradually.

By starting with two habits the first week, the goal is to establish these habits firmly before adding more. The tasks for the first week are related tasks—one leads to the next. They're all media-related, and each makes the next one easier.

Once these initial habits are established and feel like a natural part of your routine, you can start adding more habits and gradually build up to doing all seven.

If we suggested doing everything in week one, most people would get overwhelmed and give up.

When building a new habit, it's crucial to start small to avoid feeling overwhelmed.

The key to habit stacking is patience and persistence. Don't rush the process; allow each habit to become ingrained before adding more.

Over time, this approach will help you develop the skills necessary to not only grow your gym but also to maintain that growth sustainably.

Embrace habit stacking as a strategic approach to skill development. By consistently practicing and refining these habits, you'll create a strong foundation for your business and ensure its long-term success.

PHASE 3

MAINTAINING MOMENTUM

The most powerful force in business is momentum. The Golden Hour is designed to help you build momentum quickly each day, by starting the day with a small win.

When you successfully complete a full week, you'll build massive momentum.

Soon, these tasks will become daily habits and then they'll become skills.

You'll know that you're developing skills when you don't struggle to get started in the morning, and you can go weeks at a time without missing a day.

At first, though, you'll have to fight to make time and space to complete the tasks. Maybe they'll take longer than planned. Maybe some obstacle will get in your way: if you've never logged into your Google Business Profile before, you might have to spend 10 minutes learning how to do it.

If you miss a day, don't try to catch up.

Write the day off, but be absolutely certain to make the next day. Never, ever miss two days in a row. Over time, your misses will become less frequent.

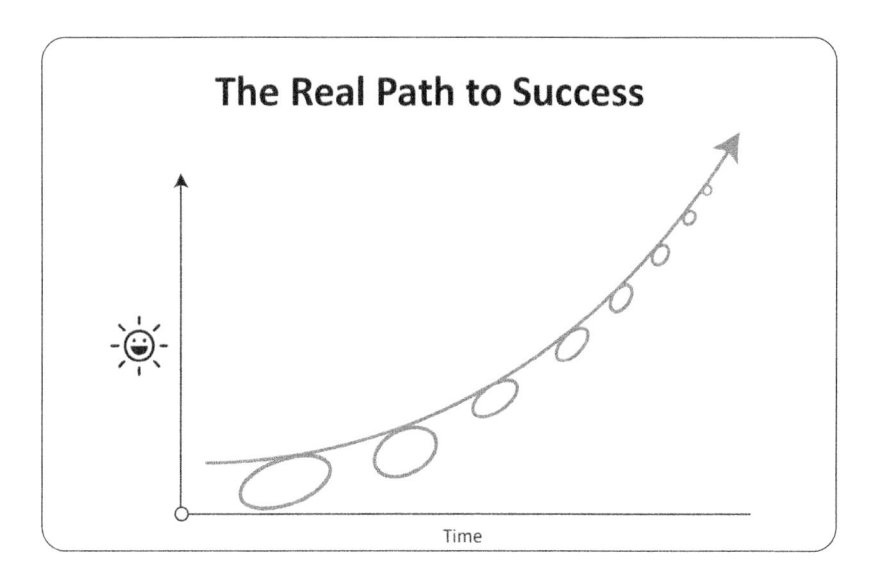

The Real Path to Success

Time

Real businesses don't grow in a straight line. At first, it can feel like you're taking one step forward, and one step back again. But if you keep practicing these habits, you'll soon be taking two steps forward to every one step back; and then three; and then four, etc.

Someday, you'll notice that you've completed a whole month or more consistently—but that doesn't mean you can move on to something different.

The point of this book is that you can't ever stop doing the basics daily. As I write this, my streak for daily actions is 172 days long. That doesn't mean I'll be perfect forever, but I'm on a good roll. Eventually, I'll miss a day; and then I'll start a new streak.

The real meta-skill of resilience doesn't mean that you never stop; it means that you restart quickly after a stop.

That's why we ask you to complete a momentum tracking chart for at least your first six weeks with the Golden Hour.

What Kills Your Momentum

One reason most entrepreneurs are overwhelmed is that we're exposed to infinite novelty.

Every day, we see new ideas online. Or we'll read someone's post about doing something differently than we're currently doing, and change direction. We hear a podcast and immediately pivot our strategy, or read a new book and drop everything to try what we've learned. And we stay with that only until we finish the next book.

Or... we just get bored.

But the truth is that the best businesses keep repeating what they know works instead of trying new things all the time.

Every change in your business will slow your growth. This is because it takes time to learn the new thing; time to get good at the new thing; time to teach the new thing to your coaches; time for them to get good at it...

Sometimes those changes are worth it in the long term. But once you find something that works for your business, you must keep doing it until it stops working.

- Even when it's boring.
- Even when it feels repetitive.
- Even when you read a new book, listen to a new podcast, or find a sexy new idea.

Remember: your business should be run scientifically, but it can't always be an experiment. When you find something that works, keep doing it until it stops working.

Most clinical studies take YEARS to know the results. Most gym owners give up after one or two social media posts.

Avoiding "One and Done" Thinking

This habit of moving on to new ideas too quickly can be called "one-and-done" thinking. Let me give you an example of how this can be damaging.

When new gyms start in our program, we teach them how to make social media posts. They can literally copy and paste them onto Facebook or Instagram or wherever they want.

We use a "jab-jab-jab-right hook" strategy: three posts to build interest and attention, then one post with a clear call to action.

The "jabs" feed the algorithm, build the audience, and just make sure your "right hook" will land. The "right hook" asks people to do something, like book an NSI or DM the gym owner.

We give gym owners ten "jab" posts to choose from. They can literally copy and paste them onto Facebook or Instagram or wherever they want. Then we give them a specific "right hook", called a 5130 post. A 5130 looks like this:

> *"I'm looking for 5 women in Sault Ste. Marie who want to lose 10lbs in the next 30 days."*
>
> *5 people—1 goal—30 days = 5130.*

It works enormously well. Gym owners in our program use it to start generating interest from their audience, and they usually book a few NSIs and earn the money to pay for the first month of our program.

They share that it's worked, they're excited, they're happy: "Two-Brain works!" They feel like they've started to build some momentum. They celebrate their 5130 post with their mentor and with a post in our private groups.

But many never do it again!

Instead of putting a working strategy on 'repeat', they ask "what's next?"

Hey, I get it—I constantly have to stop myself from chasing novelty.

We can all be guilty of 'one and done' thinking. Even when something is successful, we never repeat it—instead, we look for the next thing. We've developed a bias for novelty: the last thing we read is the wisest, most correct thing ever. Social media speeds this process up.

But we have a mantra on our mentor team: *"We need to be reminded more than we need to be taught."*

So instead of brainstorming, and bringing new ideas to their clients every single month, a mentor's job is to first build a plan that includes all of the elements that have worked for the client in the past.

If a "Bring a Friend Night" netted a gym three new clients last year, the mentor is going to tell the gym owner to run their Bring a Friend Night every quarter.

Instead of replacing Bring a Friend Night with some new, untested idea, they're going to get better at promoting Bring a Friend Night, and try to get four new clients from it next time. They get better at the thing that worked, instead of trying to find something new.

Now, do we introduce new stuff in Two-Brain? Yes—after it's been thoroughly tested by many gyms and proven to work better than what we've been doing.

This requires a huge data set and a scientific testing process that's really hard to do by yourself in one gym. And that's exactly why we do it: if your gym is what pays for your groceries, it shouldn't also be your science experiment. If you're constantly trying new things, you're always placing yourself at the start of another growth curve (learning, practicing, teaching, having your staff practice) and thereby slowing your growth significantly.

What really grows your business is doing the same things over and over, and doing more of those few things... instead of doing a bunch of different things all the time.

Of course, the things you repeat have to WORK—which is why you need to audit what you're doing, or trust a mentor who uses data to prove what's working, instead of just constantly jumping from new thing to new thing.

A good general rule is to spend 90% of your time repeating what works, and 10% of your time trying new things.

Control the 'tests' for new things: take a scientific approach. Track your metrics: did the new tactic measurably improve anything, or was it just something new for the sake of being different?

When something DOES work better than what you're currently doing, adopt it and stop doing the other thing. This is how you run your business scientifically.

If you're a gym owner, we do all of this research and testing for you in Two-Brain Business. You don't have to turn your gym into a test tube.

That means we identify what works, and your job is to REPEAT it CONSISTENTLY week after week.

That's how we developed the list of marketing "Reps" that we suggest you should do as part of your Golden Hour Challenge. In time, our mentors might change the specific tasks they recommend, but you'll keep the skill forever.

This is what really builds momentum. Spending 15 minutes on these each day is the marketing that grows your business.

106 THE GOLDEN HOUR

If all you can manage, on a given day, is to keep up your marketing habit, your business will keep growing. When the marketing stops, your business slowly coasts to a stop.

PHASE 4

TURN HABITS INTO SKILLS

One of the main reasons the Golden Hour is so powerful is that it helps start and develop some of the essential SKILLS of highly successful gym owners.

These were the skills that helped me turn my failing gym into a success and to make it the basis for the world's top mentoring company for gym owners.

They are also the skills I identified as being critical to the success of the top 12.5% of our mentoring clients, including the more than 50 who have become millionaires as a result.

When we looked at the top performers, two of the top skills we identified were FOCUS and DELIBERATE ACTION.

Focus is defined as the ability to block out the things we should NOT be doing. When it comes to deliberate action, even smart people procrastinate and overthink. The key to success is doing what needs to be done— particularly the CEO work.

The peak entrepreneurial skill is VIRTUOSITY—the pursuit of getting better and better at being a CEO, and focusing on making every part of your business better, instead of constantly changing the business.

The key to developing skills like these is putting in place the right HABITS that you repeat consistently.

Our data shows that clients with these solid skills outperform everyone else, even when they're given the SAME strategies and tactics as everyone else.

Skills become more valuable over time, because:

- A little bit of each skill is helpful, but a high skill level pays off even more.
- No one can copy them—they're an unassailable advantage.
- The government can't tax you on them.
- You don't lose them. If one business fails, these skills will build the next faster.
- They can be improved regardless of outcome (if you win, you learn; if you lose, you learn).
- They multiply your other investments.
- The time and effort invested to learn them has lifelong returns.

For example, focus is a skill that will multiply your return on mentorship. As I wrote earlier in this book, the gym owners who get the best ROI in our mentorship program often say "I just did what my mentor told me." And the owners who get the lowest ROI often say, "I'm just too busy to do the work!"

Of course, both groups have nearly the same amount of work, but the top-earners have the skill of focus.

Another important skill is developing a mindset of abundance: many business owners pass over opportunities to collaborate because they see only competition.

Instead of worrying about "share of wallet" and trying to build our own software or insurance companies, we commonly link to vendors we really like and focus on being the best at mentorship. For a gym owner, this might mean collaborating with a local physical therapist and focusing on delivering the best client outcomes through coaching, instead of trying to learn rehab and 'compete' with the professionals.

Another example of a specific business-related skill is public speaking. I have a coach for this particular skill. If every business that I own tanked overnight, I would use this skill to rebuild from scratch. Ditto blogging and podcasting. These skills don't go away when the market changes or you get your pricing structure wrong.

A further important skill in business is patience. This will usually pay off with your investments. Given a long enough timeline, real estate almost always pays off, and stock markets trend upward. Warren Buffett has said, "If you aren't willing to own a stock for 10 years, don't even think about owning it for 10 minutes."

Clearly, this principle works in the pursuit of fitness itself: learning how to squat, press and deadlift properly will make all future forms of exercise more effective.

Getting the Right Balance

Of course, it's also important to be doing the right things. That means getting the right balance between consistently performing the regular activities that are essential to growing your business (usually marketing related) with making time to work on the longer term projects that will determine its long-term success. You have to lift the roof and the floor, or your business will leap upward and fall all the way back down to ground level again.

I've been teaching these skills for years and they are core to our mentoring program.

But I realized I'd never brought them together in a way that made it easy for people to put them at the heart of their daily activity.

For that to work I had to find a way to allocate the tasks that need to be done— both every day repeating tasks and longer term project work—and also make sure that people do them in the best way possible.

That's why I decided to formalize the concept of the Golden Hour so that it would help people develop these skills, while also becoming the essential way to start your day if you want to succeed.

For example, while most gym owners are scouring the Internet for the latest marketing hack, or listening to a 30-minute podcast on selling high-ticket offers, or reading a book about leadership, the best gym owners are asking, "How can I make my lead nurture process faster?"

Here's the real key to growth in your business that most don't understand:

Master the basics yourself. Systemize them for your staff.

Optimize outcomes over time, but do the basics forever.

I mentioned virtuosity and it is one of the hardest skills for entrepreneurs to practice. Yet, it's simply a mastery of the fundamentals instead of trying every new idea that comes along.

High-level performers in golf, for example, work on their basic swing for years; novices buy new equipment.

This is true in most sports. Greg Glassman, founder of CrossFit, used the gymnastics definition of virtuosity: performing the common uncommonly well.

For example, a gym owner should work to master their skill in selling their program before attempting to "flood their gym" with marketing. But the siren song of "leads! leads! leads!" is strong enough to distract most of them.

Likewise, a gym owner should develop their staff to make them all an 8/10 as coaches, instead of employing a few "3s" and one "9". This includes evaluations and feedback—uncomfortable processes that many gym owners forget or ignore.

Entrepreneurs in any service business should develop the skill of asking for referrals, nurturing leads, and creating content before considering a TikTok account... but most lack the discipline to master the basics, because the lure of novelty is so strong.

One of the challenges of mastering the basics is that it gets boring. Who wants to do another sales roleplay session when there are YouTube videos about the CrossFit games to watch?

It's also tempting to be the first to try (and talk about) a new idea, be an early adopter, or tell your friends how to do the new thing. This is the curse of the novice.

In a letter to coaches around the world, Glassman wrote, "There is a compelling tendency among novices developing any skill or art, whether learning to play the violin, write poetry, or compete in gymnastics, to quickly move past the fundamentals and on to more elaborate, more sophisticated movements, skills, or techniques. This compulsion is the novice's curse—the rush to originality and risk."

He went on to describe this novice's curse—manifested as "excessive adornment, silly creativity, weak fundamentals and, ultimately, a marked lack of virtuosity and delayed mastery."

This is equally true in business. Focusing on building a Facebook ads campaign before a consistent sales process means a lot of wasted time on cold leads, poor conversion and burnout.

Worse, it's hard to learn to be a better salesperson if the pitch is different every time, because the entrepreneur can't see what's working with clarity.

Mastering Essential Skills

Here are examples of some of the core skills every entrepreneur should seek to master.

- The daily marketing tactics in this book
- Reading a P&L
- Getting client referrals
- Consistent delivery of service by your staff
- Selling your product or service
- Client communications
- Staff evaluations
- Content creation

It's important to note that complete "mastery" of any of these is nearly impossible. But most entrepreneurs can grow their business faster by improving the fundamentals than by adding new strategies or tactics.

For example, even basic familiarity with a Profit and Loss (P&L) statement will help an entrepreneur understand how their business is doing.

But the pursuit of mastery—asking questions of the bookkeeper, thinking about avoiding overtaxation, identifying opportunities, and putting in lots of reps—will grow their business faster than searching for new trends on social media.

The P&L should create focus for a business owner, which is the first step to growth.

As another example, a business owner who can improve their close rate by 10% will grow their business faster than an owner who increases their ad spend by twice as much. Ads take time to ramp up; time to optimize; and require constant monitoring. When they begin to slow down, they have to be retooled and the process begins again.

But sales is different: performing better with every lead will multiply the value of all future advertising.

Yet, most entrepreneurs skip from advertising platform to platform; make small investments in each; and then move to the next when their ads "don't work".

The basics never go away. Mastering them is more important than learning something new, but the pull of novelty is strong.

Of course we can't ignore the fun new stuff. But novelty must always be balanced with the pursuit of virtuosity in the fundamentals.

Virtuosity isn't the pursuit of doing more. It's the pursuit of doing better.

The challenge is that virtuosity isn't a single-step process. That means you must be willing to constantly audit your processes, cut away excess and waste, and practice, practice, practice.

The Real Secret to Developing Skills

The key to developing skills isn't just knowing what to do. It's about having the right habits and feedback.

If you struggle with the habits, tasks and actions we talk about in this book, you should book a call with a mentor.

I'll be totally honest here. I work with a mentor to hold me accountable to building my habits:

- I have a cycling coach to write my workouts and check my progress.
- I have a nutrition coach to write my plan and check my progress.
- I have a mental coach to meet with biweekly, hear my progress, and give me assignments to improve as a leader.
- I have a business coach (actually, a few) who checks my progress and tells me which steps to take next.

Even the knowledge that you "should" have a Golden Hour each day is often not enough to build the habit, especially at first.

You probably need someone to help you start the habit and reinforce the habit.

Over time, you'll need less coaching, and accountability to keep the habit going… but you'll always need SOME coaching, some external accountability. The need will decrease over time but never go away entirely.

There are various types of mentoring but our mentorship program is front-loaded with coaching to help you build the habits—and thereby the skills—you'll need to succeed as an entrepreneur.

At first, you'll talk with your coach or mentor very frequently—often weekly in person and daily through email and text.

After a few months, you'll speak to them a little less. As you gain momentum, your long "how to" and "let's get this done" conversations will shift to future-focused conversations: planning, removing future obstacles, and working on larger projects without as much oversight.

The value of your relationship with your mentor isn't in how much time you spend together—it's measured by the outcomes you create together.

Though you'll gradually come to spend less time with your mentor, that time will increase in value, because the scope of the projects you complete will get larger and more valuable to you and your business.

The Golden Hour helps you build your foundation. A mentor helps you lift your business to greater heights.

THE GOLDEN HOUR LITE—THE TRUTH ABOUT PRODUCTIVITY

Even if you don't feel you have an hour to spare every day, I want to emphasize the most important points about being productive.

We're ALL busy. Our problem, as entrepreneurs, is that we confuse "busyness" with progress.

It's very possible to open your gym at 6am, work straight through until 9pm, and not accomplish anything.

- ▶ Maybe you made a few dollars, but not more than the month before.
- ▶ Maybe you trained a few clients, but not more than last year on the same date.
- ▶ Maybe the gym is clean, but you didn't attract anyone else.
- ▶ Maybe the coaches got paid, but they didn't earn more—and neither did you.

In fact, it's very common for an entrepreneur to feel as if the only people benefiting from their business are the client, the landlord and the tax man.

I fell into this trap before I hit that park-bench-rock-bottom. "I'm working as hard as I can, but the business isn't growing!

I'm smarter than other people—why is their business growing, and not mine?"

Of course, this led to feelings of frustration and jealousy.

My mentor pulled me out of this rut by giving me things to do that actually grew my business.

He called my Golden Hour "working ON my business instead of working IN my business." I finally understood what that meant:

- ► The hours spent marketing, improving my systems, and applying my new knowledge were the things that grew my business (working ON it.)
- ► The hours spent coaching, cleaning, programming, and watching lifting videos did NOT grow my business (I was working IN it.)

Improving my skills as a coach didn't grow my business. Getting more certifications didn't grow my business. But writing my SOPs, reviewing my P&L, and doing my marketing work grew my business.

That was the CEO work. And it took me a while to understand that being the CEO was my actual job now. When I moved from 'trainer' to 'owner', I became CEO and took on the responsibility for growth.

But still... it was many more years before I learned the difference between hours and outcomes.

I remember a conversation with John Franklin, the future CMO of Two-Brain Business. I was still a fairly immature CEO, even though Two-Brain was growing, thanks to John's work.

We were using Slack to communicate internally, and our team was already over 30 people. So I was on Slack a LOT. I would get up at 5am, invest my Golden Hour into growing Two-Brain Business, and then spend hours responding to messages and going to meetings, as well as mentoring around 30 gym owners myself.

John didn't do that. John would get up and immediately set his phone notifications to "off". He would check in on Slack twice per day; book all of his meetings on Thursdays; and spend most of his time out of reach.

We were getting great results, but the uneducated farm kid in me still thought, deep down, "Imagine if he worked 40 hours per week at this, instead of 20!"

One day, I was frustrated about something else, and took it out on John:

> "You're never available! I send you messages and I have to wait HOURS to get a response. You're slowing down the process. You need to keep your Slack notifications turned on during working hours."

John patiently explained that while I measured "hard work" by time spent, he measured "hard work" by outcomes.

It took me a while to digest that, but he was right: spending more time on Slack, attending more meetings and responding to emails faster would NOT make him a better CMO.

It was a great example of "lifting the ceiling" on the company: I was still stuck in a mindset I'd learned in childhood (more work is better work) and needed to evolve my thinking for the company to grow.

If John had simply complied with my request, he'd have spent more time doing things that didn't grow the company, and we'd have stagnated or even stopped growing.

"Productivity" is really a measure of outcomes, not of time spent.

While this book is called the Golden Hour, and I want you to build the skill of focusing on growing your business for a full hour every day, here's the truth: if you ONLY do the 15-minute marketing tasks every day, you'll grow faster than 80% of the gyms out there.

That short time block will start to grow your business faster because it's probably more than you're currently doing to grow your gym.

That might offend you: after all, you're working a 14-hour day... right?

- But how much of that 14-hour day is spent on things that actually grow your business?
- How focused are you on marketing when you DO have an hour to invest?
- How much of that hour do you spend trying to figure out your software; how much is spent scrolling around; how much is spent learning?

How much gets DONE?

The reality is that you don't get a raise for working harder. You don't get clients by knowing more about marketing. You grow by doing. You get a raise for making your gym more profitable. You get more clients by doing marketing...not reading about it. And since almost no gym owners are good at consistent production, they're usually not productive—just busy.

The reason I emphasize these points is to make clear that even if you don't feel you can commit a full hour each day to this process, make sure you devote time each day to working ON your business. Don't get stuck working IN it. That's one of the most important factors in your growth.

FULFILLING THE GOLDEN AGE
Our opportunity and responsibility as entrepreneurs

Someday, you'll be doing your daily reflection and realize: yesterday was a pretty good day. A DAMN good day. A Golden Day!

And then someday, when you're doing BSFs and looking back on your week, you'll realize: you've had a great week! Almost flawless! Maybe one little thing, but you handled it. It was truly a Golden WEEK!

Of course, those won't happen all the time, but they'll start to happen more regularly, and someday you'll be on a call with your mentor and look back and say: "Hey, my gym grew... and I didn't really feel like I was working hard at all! I had an obstacle, but I overcame it! I grew as a leader and made more money and had time with my kids! It was... a Golden MONTH!"

And then, of course, the next month might not be all Golden, but you'll have a few Golden Days, and you'll look after the Golden Hours, and you might have a Golden Week or two... and a few months later, you'll have another Golden Month!

Then, at your birthday party someday, you'll take a few moments to reflect on the year, and realize: it's been a damn good year! One for the ages! Big things happened! You're a better person than you were 12 months ago! It's been a Golden YEAR!

And in a few decades, you'll be sitting around with your friends, maybe after a pickleball game, laughing and drinking coffee, or watching your grandkids play on your lawn. And like a thunderbolt, it will hit you: you're living a Golden LIFE.

Thanks to a lifetime of fitness, your health is terrific. And thanks to your lifetime of entrepreneurship, your wealth provides more than you'll need. If you're like me, you'll look around and think: *"How did an awkward teenager who happened to pick up a barbell end up HERE?!"*

How did you produce this Golden AGE in your life, when you have health and wealth, success and a happy outlook, and lots of time?

I hope you remember that you got there by working diligently on your Golden Hours, and building up from there.

But I also hope you remember that not everyone gets the opportunity to build their own Golden Age.

A Golden Age requires you to have health and wealth at the same time.

Hopefully, your Golden Age will start early and end late. You'll become wealthy while still young, and stay healthy until you're very old.

So you've achieved enough wealth that you don't have to go into work anymore. You have time and financial freedom, and you still have enough health to have full physical autonomy. You can basically do whatever you want, because you're fit and healthy enough to do that.

The Golden Age of Your Parents

A good example of a Golden Age is your parents. Your parents probably worked three, four decades. They got to the age of 60 or

65, and they had enough savings or retirement funds or pension or whatever, that they didn't have to go to work anymore.

For the first time in their life, they had time freedom, they didn't have the nine to five, they didn't have the shift at the factory.

And they had financial freedom because their income was coming from their wealth, their savings, their retirement plan, or their pension. They had health and wealth at the same time.

Now, your parents probably had, or are having, a Golden Age that lasts maybe five to seven years. When they retired, they were probably around 65 years old. They probably had a health condition or two.

So, while they had wealth and health at the same time, that window in which they had both was pretty short—five to seven years.

They retire at 65 and they've got a little bit of extra money, a little bit of extra time, and they're fairly fit. They can play golf every day if they want to and they can hold up to that. They can bend over and do their gardening or whatever. They can buy a little place in Boca or they can buy a little sailboat. They're physically autonomous enough to do all these things.

Then, within about five to seven years, maybe their health starts catching up with them. Maybe the bad back that they started suffering in their 30s prohibits them from traveling as much anymore.

Maybe their mental acuity isn't as sharp and they can't travel on their own anymore. So they sell that little place down in Boca and their world starts getting smaller and smaller and smaller.

And before you know it, they still have enough wealth to pay their bills, but they don't have the health to enjoy it.

Five to seven years. That's their Golden Age. That's what they get for decades of working. It doesn't seem like a lot.

But compared to their parents, that's astronomical. It's amazing.

Because your grandparents probably worked right until the day they died or until the day that they physically could not work anymore.

If they were able–by some miracle–to save enough money to stop working, or they had some kind of pension where they could just stop working, they weren't really fit enough to enjoy it.

Maybe they would walk with their friends or go to the classes at the Seniors Hall. Maybe.

In my case, by the time all four of my grandparents weren't making an income anymore it was because they couldn't work anymore.

One grandfather was a farmer. He worked till the day he died. The other grandfather was a delivery guy who retired one day and the next day he started sitting in his chair and watching "The Price is Right" and "Wheel of Fortune." And that was it.

They worked hard their whole lives until they couldn't work anymore. They had no real Golden Age. But they were often content to rest. And some retirees even talk about "the Golden Years." I'm sure you've heard that before.

Because though we might view that type of "retirement" as boring or unfulfilling, the reality is that your grandparents had it a lot better than their parents did.

Their parents were born in an age when possibly one of their brothers or sisters got extremely sick, or maybe died of smallpox or some other disease that we have a vaccine for now.

They probably survived the depression and wars. They probably emigrated and made a massive life change leaving family behind. Their life was hardship and the way they measured the success of their life was just setting up the next generation to work as hard as they could. And that was your grandparents.

Your grandparents' goal was to work as hard as they possibly could to set up the next generation. They did that by being able to put them through university so they could get a better and safer job that didn't wear them out and they could start to accumulate some wealth. And your parents did that.

Your parents went to school and they got these career jobs and they stayed in the same career for 30 or 40 years. Even if they changed jobs, they were always doing the same work for decades.

Sometimes it was boring and sometimes they hated their boss and sometimes they hated their job. But they did that to set you up to take risks to give you a financial and familial safety net that would allow you to do what you're doing right now—being an entrepreneur and taking risks.

In fact, the last 2,000 generations of humanity have been building to this point to lift you up into the opportunity to have a Golden Age.

You are going to reach wealth by age 50. And you're going to stay in health longer. And that Golden Age when you have both wealth and health at the same time is going to last probably 30 years. This is so big compared to anything that's ever happened before that it's really important that we plan for it.

What will you do with this Golden Age of health and wealth?

Well, I asked the most successful gyms in our program and—no surprise!—they had a plan.

- ► They'd maintain their health.
- ► They'd help others do the same by opening more gyms.
- ► They'd learn to play guitar or speak another language.
- ► They'd make art.
- ► They'd read.
- ► They'd pray or meditate.
- ► They'd walk the dog.
- ► They'd work to benefit humanity.

The Golden Age is the time of life when the great innovators emerge. Historically, "geniuses" such as Galileo, Plato and Leonardo da Vinci were sponsored or had patrons. Darwin had an uncle who paid for his passage on the HMS Beagle. Mozart lived at the castle with his sponsor. Vaccines are now usually produced by scientists working in labs sponsored by pharmaceutical companies or governments.

We can be our **own** sponsor. We can buy our own research or pay for our own period of discovery.

For me, the Golden Age is the Thief Phase I wrote about in "Founder, Farmer, Tinker, Thief." This is where I get to play Robin Hood, make lots of money and give it away. I do that through donations and mentorship.

For you, a Golden Age might be Queen Phase, Pirate Phase, Zen Master Phase or Writer Phase.

We can be self-sponsored. We can create a new era of enlightenment. We can do almost anything.

But we can't waste the opportunity.

We did not come this far to sit on the couch and watch sitcoms.

Your parents worked for years to pay for college, they worked through college, and then they stuck with a job they often hated for decades. They saved every extra dollar and hoped to retire at age 65 with a few years of mediocre health left to them. *They did that for you.*

Their parents ground away at hard labor, missing meals, doing without, tightening their belts, scrimping and saving and trying to teach their kids about hard times. They worked until they literally couldn't work anymore, trading their sweat for a wage. *They did that for you.*

Their parents were tough people who packed only what they could carry, took great risks to find a better life, worked menial jobs, slept outdoors and were satisfied just to put a roof over their heads before they died. *They did that for you.*

Their own parents were serfs, haulers, sailors or penniless laborers. Some were slaves. They fought to survive. But they did. *And they did it for you.*

Their parents were villagers, nomads, wanderers.

They lived hand to mouth, with no idea where their next meal would come from, or when. They battled starvation, disease, exposure, abuse and weather. Nature tried to kill them every single day.

But it didn't. They held on. *And they did that for you.*

Each of these people existed at billion-to-one odds. And the odds of you existing are so remote—literally 1,000,000,000,000 to one—that it's virtually impossible. The odds are so infinitely long that they might be called divine or supernatural. And yet here you are.

The Opportunity

Now the poorest person in the Western Hemisphere has access to resources and information beyond a king's wildest dream only a few generations ago.

Thanks to innovations such as a free-market economy and democracy, we can build wealth fast enough to live in secure, safe worlds.

Even better, we can actually stop working and still survive. We can build up a horde of money and have enough to relax for a decade or two at the end of our lives.

And, for the first time, we can use money to buy time:

- ▶ We can accumulate an abundance of wealth so fast that we can stop working while we still have our health.
- ▶ We can accumulate resources that build more resources for us.
- ▶ We can stop working at a younger age and survive longer than ever before.

But this ease has led to new problems. The killers of our generation are the problems of abundance: For the first time in history, we have too much. Life's too easy, and it's hurting us.

While our lifespan continues to extend, our health span is shortening. More and more, the last few years of our lives are beset by chronic health problems such as disease and immobility.

We can survive to age 90—triple the life expectancy of our great-great-grandparents—but the last 20 years are often bad. Some regret reaching an advanced age. Without health and freedom, they can become depressed. Instead of enjoying the freedom they've created, retirement becomes the worst years of their lives.

Here's what should happen:

1. You accumulate enough wealth to stop working at a young age (while you still have good health).
2. You keep good health for as long as possible and die in your sleep after a full day of skiing with your spouse and friends.

Between those two points, your life in your Golden Age is full of laughter, experience and a sense of purpose that you're making things better for your kids. We know how to extend lifespan.

We know how to stay healthy almost right up till the end. And we know how to build wealth. But most don't do it because it's complicated. Or it was. Now it's not. And there's no excuse for failure.

Your Golden Age

When you reach your own Golden Age, I hope you do these four things:

1. **Tell people how you got there. Be a model for others.**
2. **Make lots of money and give it away.**

Earlier, I wrote about how wealth is demonized even in cultures built on wealth. The true story is that our democracy, our healthcare system, and even our mostly peaceful way of life is built on the wealth created by entrepreneurship.

When you become good at making money, you can solve your own problems. But when you become great at making money, you can solve problems for other people.

I often tell my kids that "if money solves your problem, you don't have a problem." There are many charitable people in the world; people who are willing to dedicate their time—even their entire lives!—to serve others. But these people are often limited in their ability to help because they don't have money.

Think about Mother Teresa. She lived in the streets of Calcutta with the poorest of the poor for much of her life. She did collect donations, yes, and used those donations to help the sick and the starving and the infirm. But what if she'd had a billion dollars to spend?

Now think about Bill Gates. He spent much of his life in luxury. He never went hungry. But when he retired, he had enough money to buy vaccines for 6,000,000 kids in sub-Saharan Africa. Who made the larger contribution?

Of course, they both did. There's no scoreboard for helping people. We need both the people who are willing to serve and help, and the people who are good at making money to pay the bills.

Money doesn't solve every problem, but it solves the money problems, and when access to vaccines or food is a money problem, you can solve it better than someone willing to starve with the starving.

3. Mentor others.

Dedicate some of your time and attention to helping others achieve health and wealth.

4. Open more gyms.

The value of this one is obvious: help more people extend THEIR healthspan, lifespan and wealth. Not everyone should be an entrepreneur. But everyone deserves to live a healthier, wealthier life. Lead the way.

This could be the Golden Age of our species. Instead, we're going backward. It's up to us—the fitness entrepreneurs—to turn the tide. We do that one pebble at a time: one daily action, one habit, one skill. One new lead, one new client, one life changed forever.

Thank you for your service. Stay Golden,

Coop

APPENDIX 1

HOW TO PUBLISH A BLOG POST OR QUICKCAST

Open your website dashboard. If your website is built on Wordpress, the dashboard is probably available at [website]/wp-admin. For example, if your business website is BobsGym.com, you can probably reach your website dashboard at bobsgym.com/wp-admin.

If your site is hosted on something other than Wordpress, use Google to find out how to publish a new blog post on that platform. For example, Google "Create new blog post wix" if your site is hosted on Wix.

Click "Posts" and then "Add New Post".

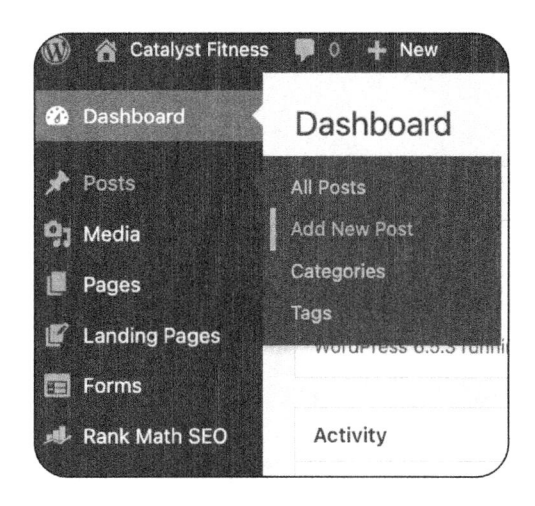

In the Title bar, type "Why I Started [your business]".

Then write the simple story of why you started your business.

Speak from the heart. Don't lapse into corporate-speak, like "We saw a need for greater quality initiatives in the fitness industry…" Tell the story of your flooded basement, the story of quitting your job as an apprentice, the story of going out solo. Why?

Don't worry if you're not good at this. Nobody is. Your fans will love your imperfections.

Write 250-400 words.

> **Why I Started Catalyst Fitness**
>
> I wasn't an athlete in high school. I was a nerd.
>
> I wasn't good at sports; didn't have much self-confidence; and would probably have chosen playing video games over going to a party with friends on a Friday night.
>
> If you'd told that skinny, introverted kid that he'd be speaking to thousands of people from stage; own multiple businesses; and write to 40,000 readers every day...he'd have thought you were nuts.
>
> The road from there to here started with a simple question:
> "Wanna see if the weight room is open?"
>
> I had a weird lunch hour - from 10am until 11am. Only a few other seniors had the same break time. Bored, one suggested that we poke around the school weight room - a windowless dungeon containing a weight stack from the 1970s and some busted up equipment that people had donated from their unused home gyms.

Before you hit Publish:
Select a blog category—probably the default.

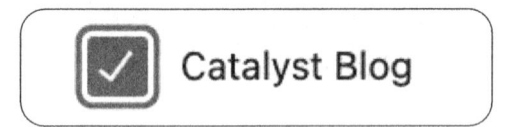

☑ Catalyst Blog

Pick a picture. Ideally, one of you.

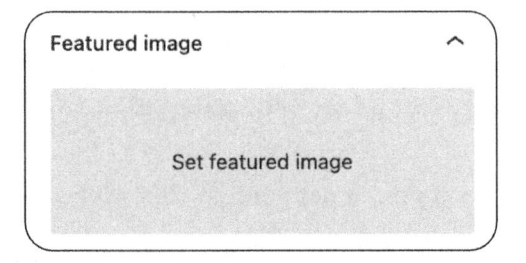

Featured image ˄

Set featured image

Add a few tags—these are the terms people search for when they're seeking information. You'll probably use the same ones almost every day. This isn't a critical step. Don't spend a lot of time on it.

Tags

ADD NEW TAG

catalyst ✕   exercise ✕
fitness ✕   gym ✕
sault ste marie ✕   workout ✕

Add a one-sentence summary in the "Excerpts" section. This isn't critical either.

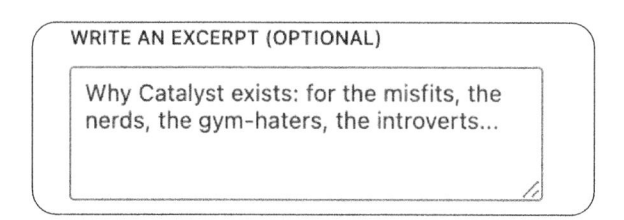

WRITE AN EXCERPT (OPTIONAL)

Why Catalyst exists: for the misfits, the nerds, the gym-haters, the introverts...

Hit "Publish".

Publish

Congrats—you've been published on the internet!

Of course, no one will see your work yet...not until we share it in the places where people are looking. That's what social media and your email list is for.

Content Ideas

Here are more questions you can ask yourself—or have someone ask you—to create some blog posts or QuickCasts.

1. What makes your gym different from others in the area?
2. Describe the range of services and programs offered at your gym.
3. How would you describe the values of your gym?
4. How do you recruit new coaches for your gym?
5. What kind of onboarding process do new members go through?
6. What qualifications and experience do your coaches have and how do they keep developing?
7. How do you keep your fitness programs up-to-date and effective?
8. What types of group classes do you offer, and how are they organized?
9. What's your approach to client assessment and goal setting for health and fitness?
10. How important is nutrition in your fitness programs, and do you offer guidance on nutrition?
11. How do you adapt your coaching to suit clients with different fitness levels and abilities?
12. What strategies do you use to keep clients motivated and engaged?
13. How do you ensure the safety and well-being of your clients during workouts?
14. How do you track and measure client progress?

15. How do you help clients with specific health conditions or injuries?
16. What is your philosophy about mental health and mindset in health and fitness?
17. How do you stay up-to-date with the latest research and trends in the world of health and fitness?
18. What types of equipment do you have, and how do you maintain them?
19. What is your philosophy about the role of personal training versus group classes?
20. How do you build a sense of community among your members?
21. What common misconceptions about health and fitness do you encounter?
22. How do you ensure a clean and hygienic environment for your members?
23. What advice do you have for someone looking to start (or restart) their fitness journey?
24. Can you share some success stories of clients who have achieved significant results?
25. How do you help clients who struggle to get the results they want?
26. What plans do you have for expanding or improving your gym in the future?
27. How do you personally stay fit and motivated as a fitness coach?
28. What do you find most rewarding about running your own gym and helping clients achieve their fitness goals?

29. How do you support your local community?

30. What are some successes you've had or milestones you've reached in your gym?

Using AI for Content Creation

These days there is a lot of talk about using AI to help in content creation. So, should you be using AI to help write your blog posts? While you can do that, the key to good results with AI is writing good prompts.

AI adapts and improves itself quickly, but the human eye is faster: most of us can spot a blog written by ChatGPT pretty quickly.

Nevertheless, if you write good prompts, and edit the content that your AI tool creates, you can personalize it.

This is a pretty big time-saver; if AI writes the blog post for you, that's 80% of the work done. Tweak and edit, then copy and paste it onto your blog.

The only time I use AI to write a blog post is when I'm absolutely uninspired. Usually, this means I'm out of practice.

Having AI write a blog post for me gets me a quick win; and then I can build momentum from there. Don't worry about feeling as if you're "cheating" or that AI doesn't speak in "your voice" or that your blog might sound like others.

Remember, this is practice: today, use AI; tomorrow, use AI again, with edits; and in the future you'll write from scratch.

Another great use of AI is having it generate podcast and blog topics for you.

Try this prompt:

"Please give me 30 good blog topics for the owner of a CrossFit gym"

You could also try:

- *"Please give me 30 interview questions for the owner of a HIIT gym"*

Then pretend an interviewer has just asked you the question, and record the answer in your blog or on a QuickCast.

How to Record and Publish a QuickCast

Let's talk now about how to record a QuickCast.
First, open the voice recorder on your phone.

Pretend I'm interviewing you.
My first question: "Tell me the story of your business."
Hit 'record'.

> **New Recording 4**
>
> 00:01.28

Tell me the story of your business: What got you started? What were the hard parts? What got you to where you are now?

You have five minutes. End the recording when you're done. Make sure you save it with the title "The Story of My Business".

> | Cut | Copy | Look Up | Translate | > |
>
> **New Recording 4**
> 7:54 AM
>
> 0:00   −0:26

How to Publish a Blog Post or Quickcast   139

Send the recording to your laptop.

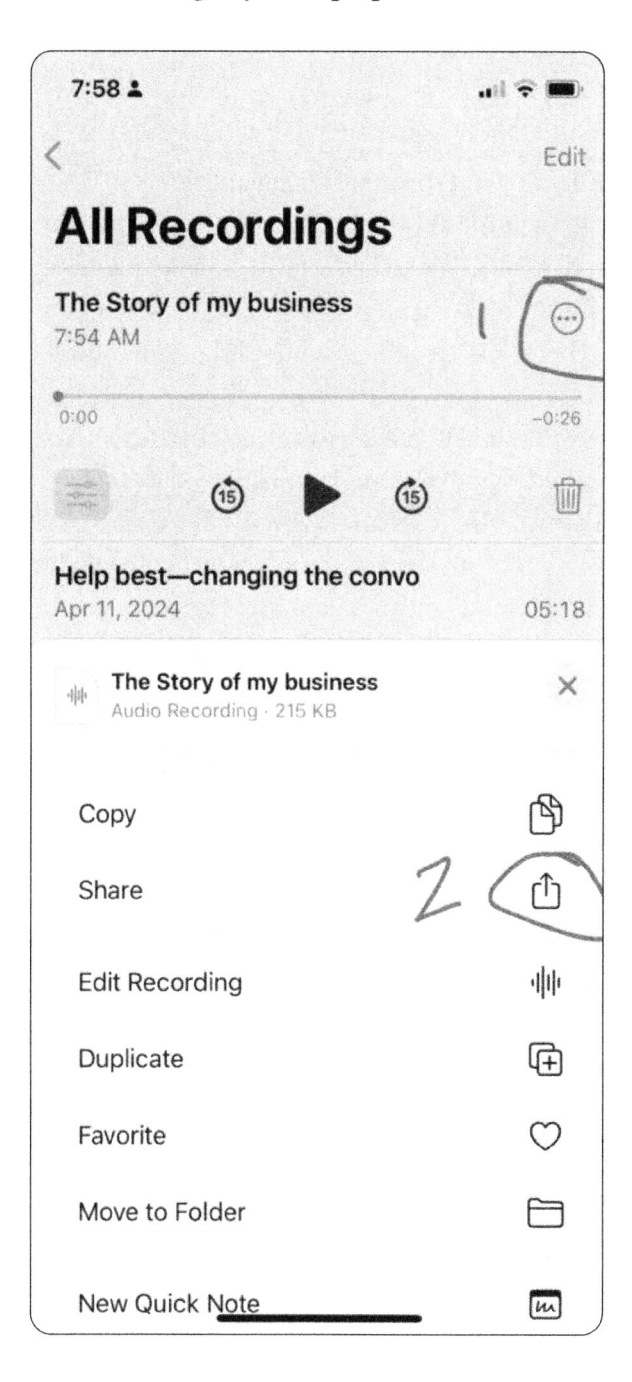

Repeat the steps for a second interview. This time, the question is:

"Why did you want to start this business?"

You don't need to talk the listener into buying from you; it's not an advertisement. It's just a story to help people relate to you. Be transparent.

Repeat the steps to name, save and send the episode to your laptop.

Tomorrow, we'll set up a distribution channel.

This is called "QuickCasting", and it's a very easy way to start brand marketing.

Today, we're going to share your QuickCast with your audience.

Open Captivate or your podcast hosting software.

Select your podcast.

Click "Copy RSS Feed".

The Catalyst

Podcast Settings   Copy RSS Feed

Open Instagram.

Click "Create", then "Post".

How to Publish a Blog Post or Quickcast 141

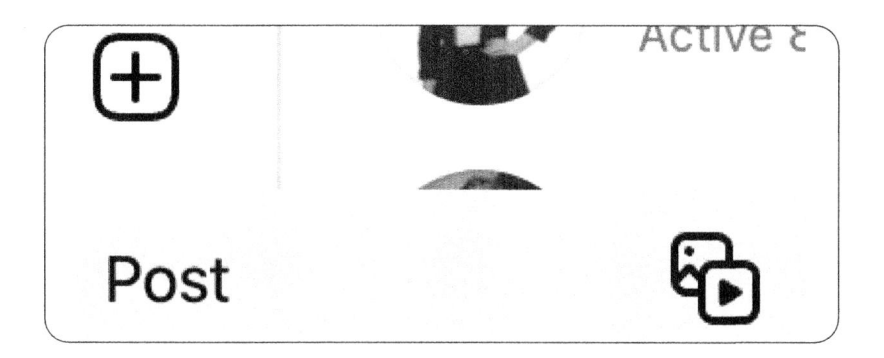

Write a short description—you don't have to be fancy. Include "link in comments" and hashtags for your business, service and city.

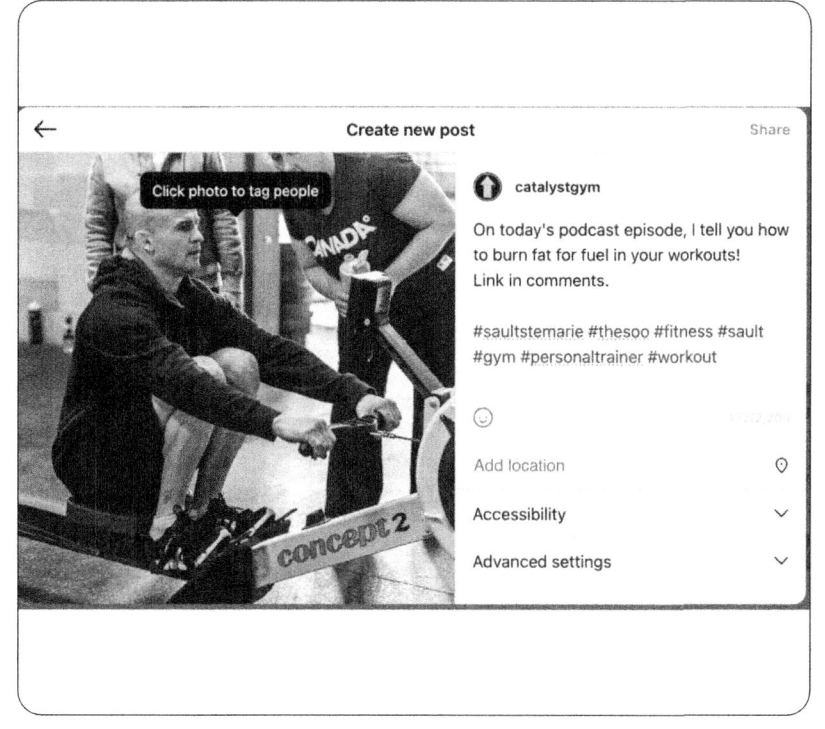

Hit "Share".
Click on the post you just made.
In the comments, enter the link to your podcast.

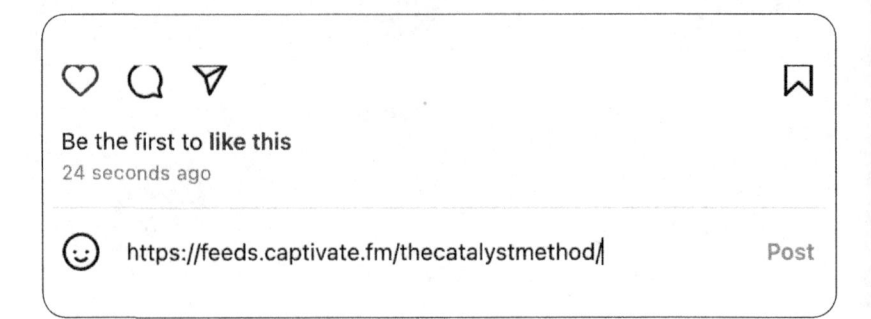

> ♡ ○ ▽   🔖
>
> Be the first to like this
> 24 seconds ago
>
> ---
>
> 🙂 https://feeds.captivate.fm/thecatalystmethod/   Post

Hit "Enter".

Now repeat this process on Facebook and LinkedIn—but on those platforms, you can share the link right in the post instead of in the Comments section. Like this:

> **Catalyst Fitness**
> 🌐 Public ▼
>
> On today's podcast episode, I tell you how to burn fat for fuel in your workouts!
> https://feeds.captivate.fm/thecatalystmethod/
>
> #saultstemarie #thesoo #fitness #sault #gym #personaltrainer #workout

Make sure you add a picture before publishing. 🙂

Then open your email software.

Click "Send email".

How to Publish a Blog Post or Quickcast 143

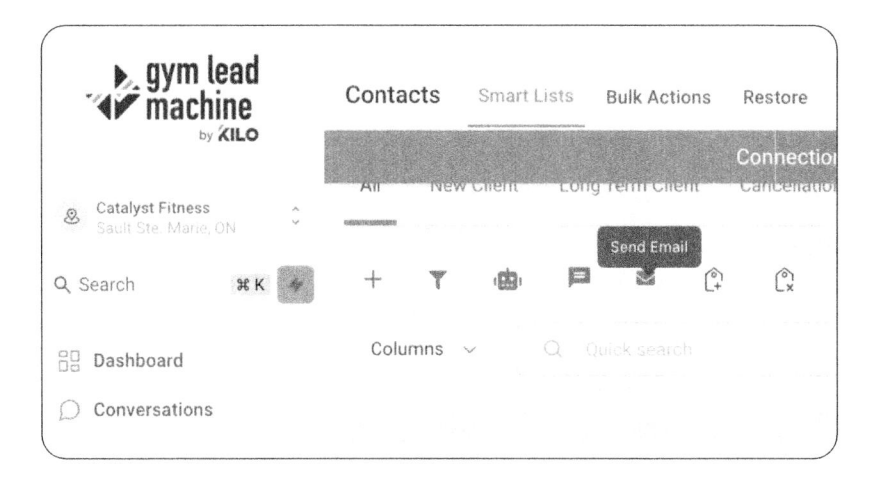

Click "select all" (or filter for people who are on your list but not part of your lead-nurture sequence.)

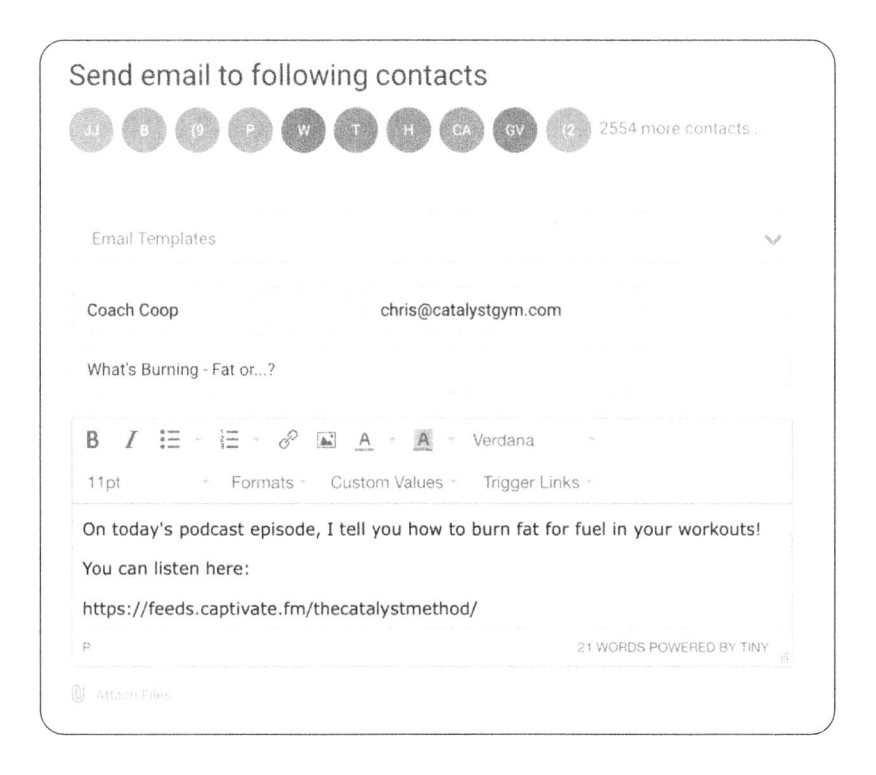

Use the same text as in your social media posts. No need to get fancy.

Hit "SEND".

Done.

Make a list of 30 interview questions and begin recording one or two QuickCasts each week. As with the first week, pretend I'm interviewing you; hit "record" on your phone; and just answer the question, even if it's a short answer.

Upload your QuickCasts and distribute them according to the "Daily Tasks" schedule.

For more detail, listen to my QuickCast about QuickCasting here: https://businessisgood.com/quickcasting/

APPENDIX 2

HOW TO DISTRIBUTE YOUR CONTENT

To get started distributing Monday's content, pull up the blog post or QuickCast you created the day before.

(In case you want to follow along, the blog post I'm using is a daily workout post from our gym site. Here it is: https://catalystgym.com/daily-catalyst/daily-catalyst-052824/)

First stop: Instagram. (We'll use the Desktop version, but you can do this on your phone if you prefer.)

Hit "Create" then "Post".

Drag a picture.

Write your caption. Don't get hung up on this. Use ChatGPT to help if you need it. Just give people a reason to follow the link you'll share next.

Add hashtags. I use the same ones every day—I just have them sitting on my Clipboard and copy them into my Instagram posts.

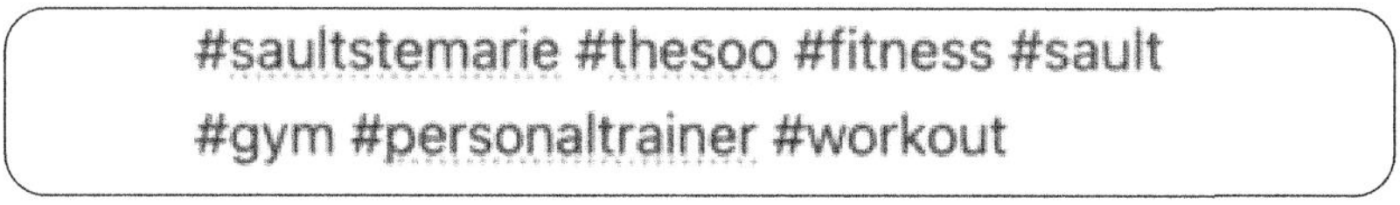

How to Distribute Your Content — 147

> #saultstemarie #thesoo #fitness #sault #gym #personaltrainer #workout

Copy your blog's URL and paste it in Comments.

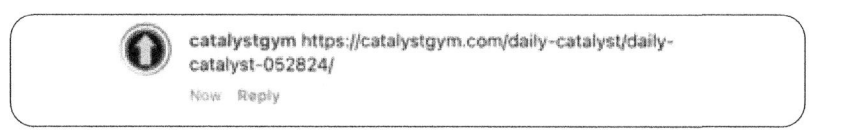

> catalystgym https://catalystgym.com/daily-catalyst/daily-catalyst-052824/
> Now Reply

Now highlight the text in your Instagram post and hit "Copy" (Command+C on a Mac.)

Open your Facebook Page. (Don't know the difference between your profile and your business page? Read here.)

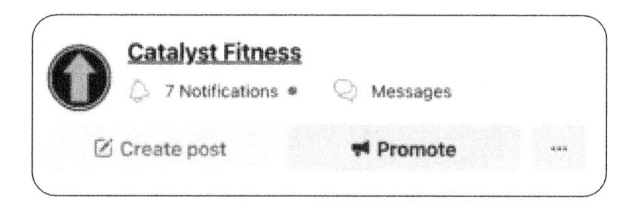

> **Catalyst Fitness**
> 7 Notifications • Messages
> Create post Promote

Hit "Create Post" (you might have to hit "Switch" to post as your Business Profile.)

Paste the text from your Instagram post into the Facebook page post.

Remove the "link in comments" line and replace it with the URL from your blog post. Facebook allows you to link directly to an off-platform address; Instagram doesn't.

148 THE GOLDEN HOUR

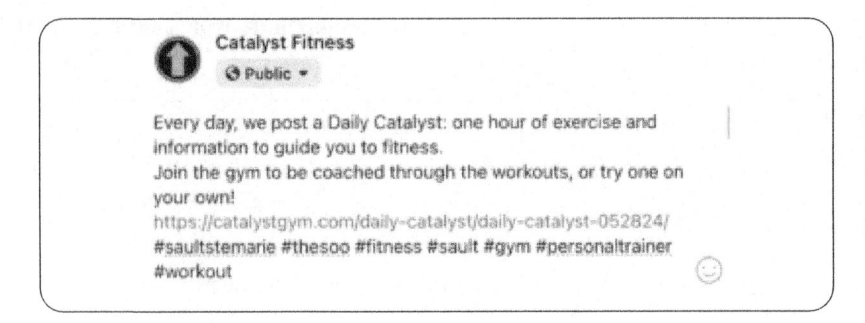

> **Catalyst Fitness**
> Public ▼
>
> Every day, we post a Daily Catalyst: one hour of exercise and information to guide you to fitness.
> Join the gym to be coached through the workouts, or try one on your own!
> https://catalystgym.com/daily-catalyst/daily-catalyst-052824/
> #saultstemarie #thesoo #fitness #sault #gym #personaltrainer #workout

Add your picture from Instagram.

Hit "Post". It should look like this. Here's a direct link to the post on the Catalyst Fitness Facebook page, in case you want to see it.

Copy all the text from your Facebook post, including the link to your blog (the URL), but not including the Hashtags.

How to Distribute Your Content   149

If you have a free public group on Facebook, open it. You might have to switch back to your personal profile first.

Share your post in your free Facebook group. Don't include the hashtags. If you have a private members' group for your business, post it there too.

Now open your Google Business Profile.

(If you can't find it, start with www.google.com/business.)

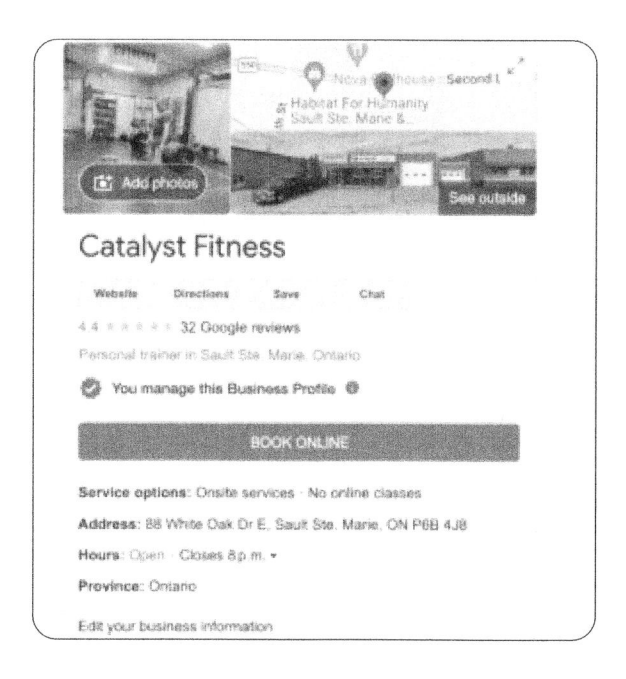

Scroll down to "Add a post".

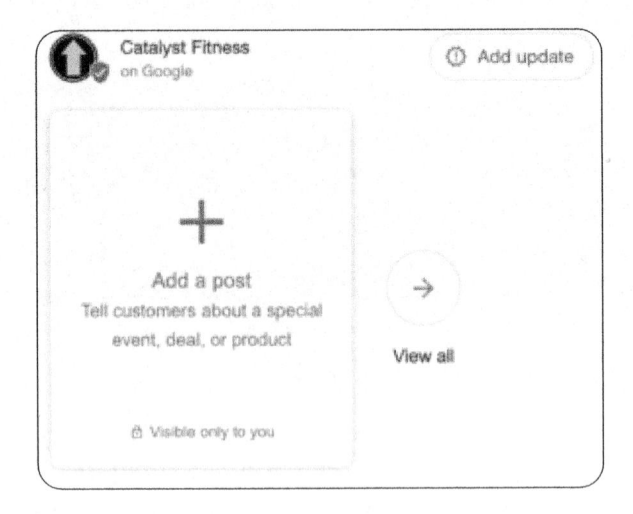

Copy your post from Facebook. Include the URL to click, and the hashtags.

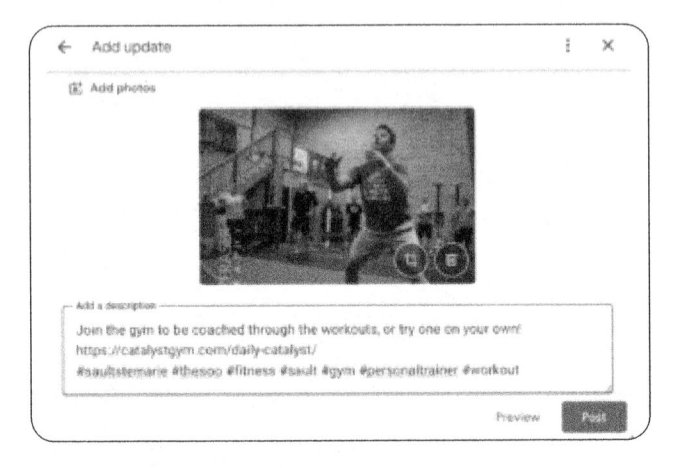

Scroll down to "Add a button (optional)".

Select "Learn More" from the dropdown menu.

Paste the URL of your blog post into the "Link for your button" space.

Hit "Post".

Now open your CRM (or whatever you use to send emails to your email list.) I'll share screenshots from Gym Lead Machine (the CRM I use for my gym) but yours could look quite different.

The goal here is to send a short email to your list. These can be longer—they don't have to be a quick link to your website. If someone's on your email list, they've probably already been to your website.

Use your email list for clearer calls to action, like "Book a free consultation"—something that moves the client from "paying attention" to "paying money".

Click "Contacts" (or however you get to your email list in your software).

Click "Send Email" (or "New Email", or however you start writing a new email in your software).

You might have to select a list of contacts first. If your email software allows you to use filters, I'd exclude everyone who's been on your list for less than 30 days.

They're probably already in an automated email sequence, so there's no purpose in interrupting your automations with another CTA. But if this is confusing, don't worry about it—send the email to everyone.

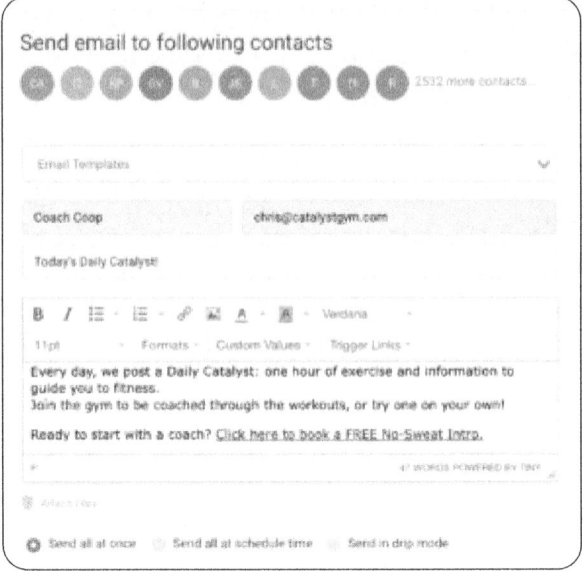

Notice the clear Call to Action (with a clickable link) at the bottom.

Hit "SEND". This probably took you a full hour. But after you practice a few times, you'll be able to do it in 15 minutes.

And you've achieved a lot: you've shared your content on three social media platforms AND to your email list.

You'll repeat this every Tuesday.

APPENDIX 3

HOW TO CHECK IN WITH YOUR CLIENTS

Your clients should have regularly-scheduled goal reviews, where you measure their progress and update their exercise and nutrition plan.

But if your clients aren't on a regular schedule yet, start by messaging 5 at a time (or 20 per month) to get them booked in for their first goal review.

Start a private message with 5 clients. If most of your clients are on Facebook, use Facebook Messenger.

Otherwise, use text.

First message: "Hey [client]! It's [coach] here from [gym]. How's it going?"

Then follow the text flowchart:

THE GOLDEN HOUR

GOAL REVIEW CHAT

How's it going?

"Amazing!"

Great to hear! What's your biggest win right now?

"I did XYZ!"

I saw that! I'm so proud of you. A lot of people would love to do that. Can I share your story?

- **"Sure!"**
  - Amazing! I'll meet you after your next session to do a little interview. Cool?
  - While I have you: Any other goals you're working on?
  - Do you have ten minutes in the next week to make a plan for these?
  - Great, here's a link to my calendar. Pick any time you like!
  - [Calendar Link]

- **"I'd rather you didn't..."**
  - Totally get it! Still proud :)
  - While I have you: Any other goals you're working on?
  - Do you have ten minutes in the next week to make a plan for these?
  - Great, here's a link to my calendar. Pick any time you like!
  - [Calendar Link]

"Pretty good, I guess."

Happy with your progress so far?

- **"Yes"**

  Great to hear! What's your biggest win right now?

  "I did XYZ!"

  I saw that! I'm so proud of you. A lot of people would love to do that. Can I share your story?

  - **"Sure!"**
    - Amazing! I'll meet you after your next session to do a little interview. Cool?
    - While I have you: Any other goals you're working on?
    - Do you have ten minutes in the next week to make a plan for these?
    - Great, here's a link to my calendar. Pick any time you like!
    - [Calendar Link]

  - **"I'd rather you didn't..."**
    - Totally get it! Still proud :)
    - While I have you: Any other goals you're working on?
    - Do you have ten minutes in the next week to make a plan for these?
    - Great, here's a link to my calendar. Pick any time you like!
    - [Calendar Link]

- **"Not really"**
  - Do you have ten minutes in the next week to measure your progress and make a new plan?
  - Great, here's a link to my calendar. Pick any time you like!
  - [Calendar Link]

"Actually, not well..."

Sorry to hear that! Let's get you back on track.

- Do you have ten minutes in the next week to measure your progress and make a new plan?
- Great, here's a link to my calendar. Pick any time you like!
- [Calendar Link]

Two-Brain Business

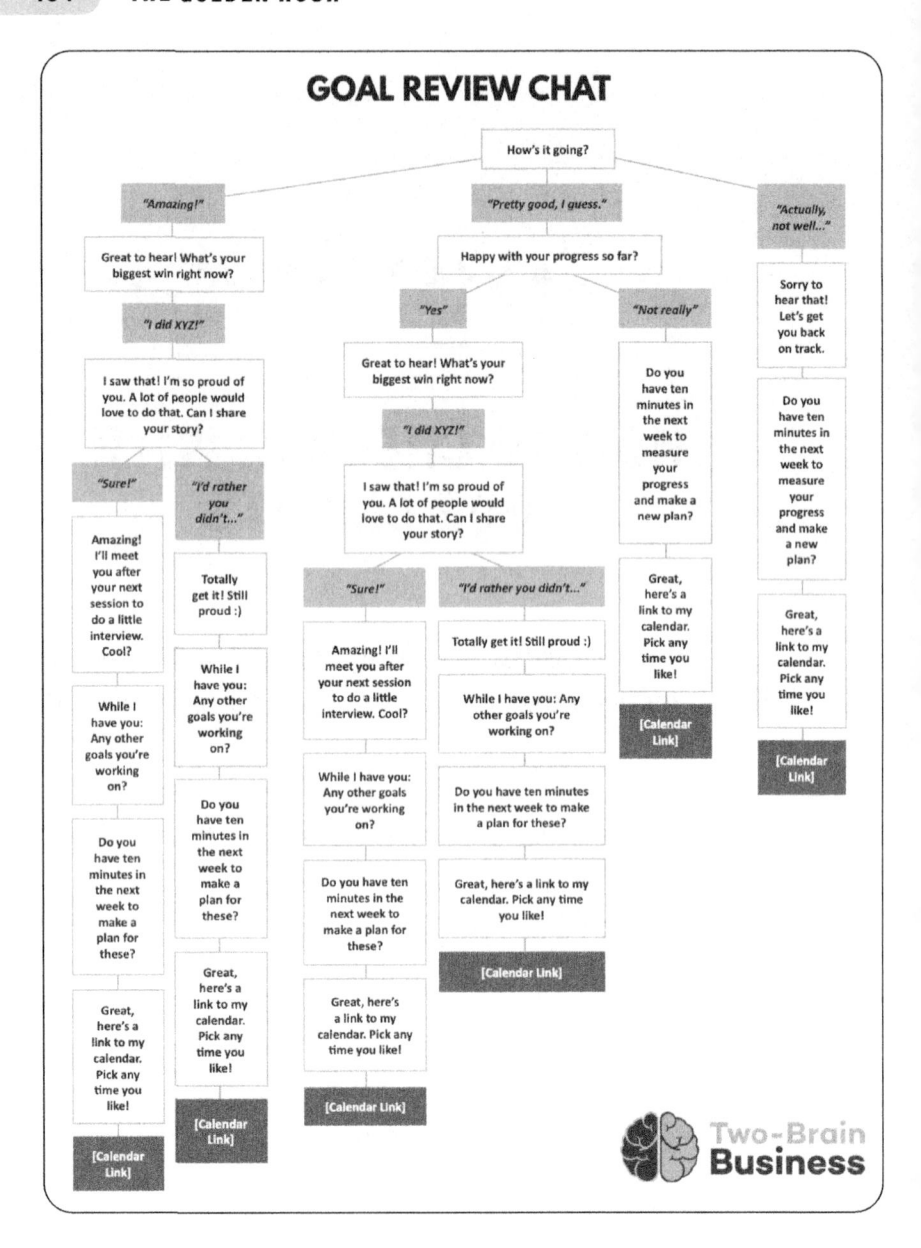

Your goal is to book 5 clients in for Goal Reviews.

When you meet with them, you'll follow the Goal Review Script.

Remember to book their next goal review before they leave their first!

APPENDIX 4

HOW TO MINE YOUR LEADS

1. **Direct Message Five Instagram Followers**

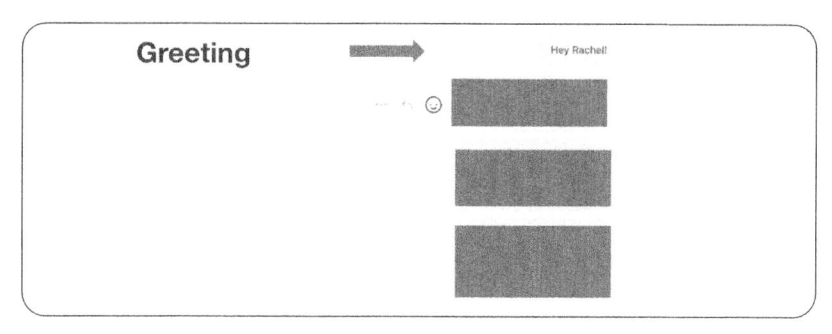

Notifications

New

eppy4417 started following you. 19m   [Follow]

Greeting ⟶ Hey Rachel!

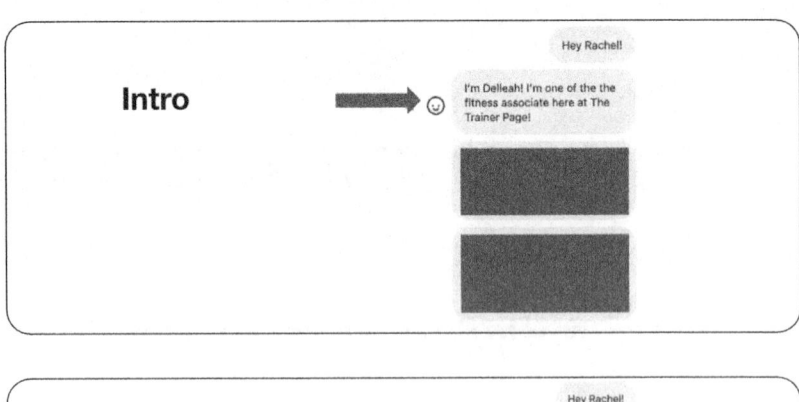

156 THE GOLDEN HOUR

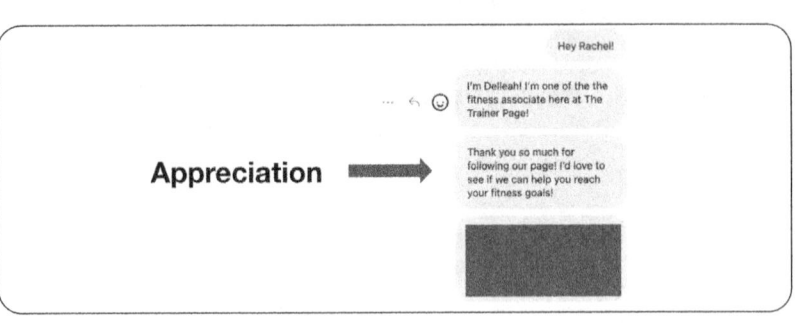

Intro

> Hey Rachel!
> I'm Delleah! I'm one of the the fitness associate here at The Trainer Page!

Appreciation

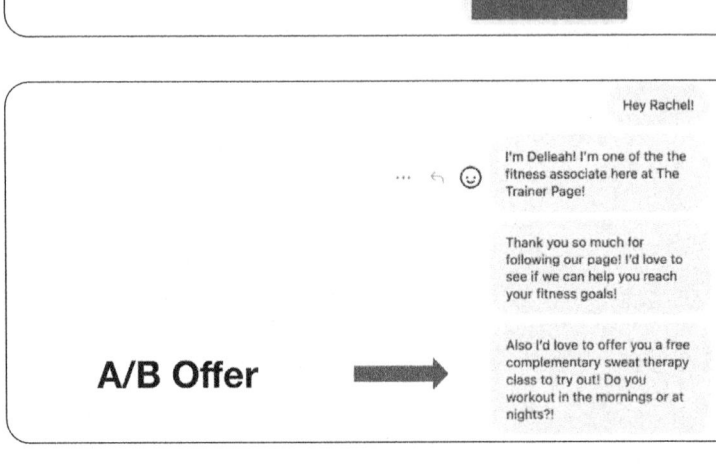

> Hey Rachel!
> I'm Delleah! I'm one of the the fitness associate here at The Trainer Page!
> Thank you so much for following our page! I'd love to see if we can help you reach your fitness goals!

A/B Offer

> Hey Rachel!
> I'm Delleah! I'm one of the the fitness associate here at The Trainer Page!
> Thank you so much for following our page! I'd love to see if we can help you reach your fitness goals!
> Also I'd love to offer you a free complementary sweat therapy class to try out! Do you workout in the mornings or at nights?!

How to Mine Your Leads   157

Handle Objections

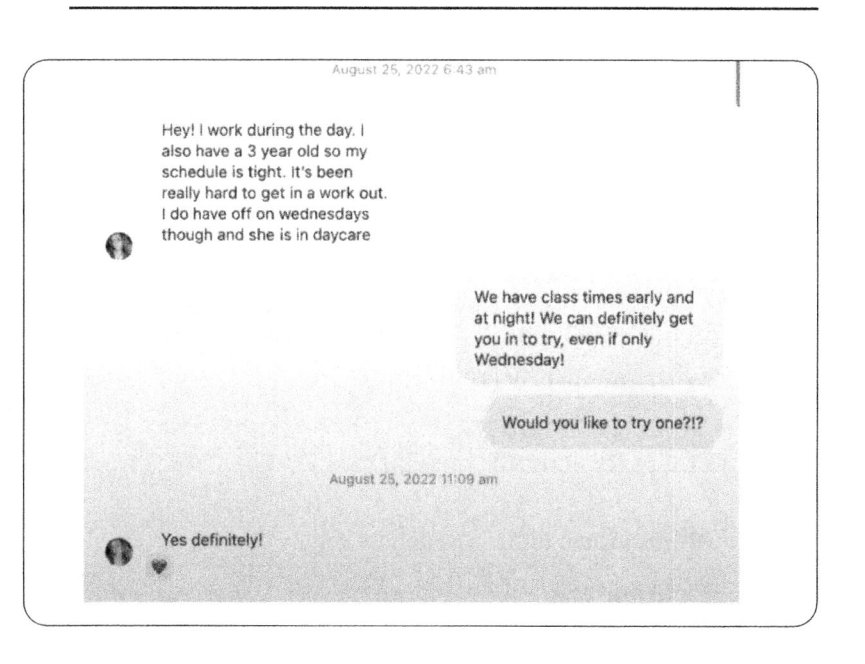

> Hey! I work during the day. I also have a 3 year old so my schedule is tight. It's been really hard to get in a work out. I do have off on wednesdays though and she is in daycare

August 25, 2022 6:43 am

> We have class times early and at night! We can definitely get you in to try, even if only Wednesday!

> Would you like to try one?!?

August 25, 2022 11:09 am

> Yes definitely!
> ♥

Move to a phone call

> Ofc! What's your full name and number we'll reach out tomorrow and set it up !!

> 7334. Thank you! Congrats on 3 years!!
> ♥

2. Email Five Former Clients

First, open your CRM or email service.

Find your "cancellations" list, if you have one. If you require clients to fill out a form when they want to cancel, you'll have a "cancellations" list. If you don't, that's okay—this will just take a bit longer.

Scroll through your email list. Find five clients who have canceled (but you'd love to have them back.) It might be best to start with the oldest email addresses first (sort in reverse chronological order).

Send them this email:

- **Subject line:** *Quick Question*
- **Email body:** *Are you still interested in [what your service does] in [year]?*

For example, write "Are you still interested in improving your fitness in 2024?" instead of "Are you still interested in buying a gym membership in 2024?"

Focus on the benefits of your service instead of its features. If you have notes from the client, use their specific goals.

For example, if the client came in asking to improve their strength, use that in the email body:

"Are you still interested in getting stronger in 2024?"

Hit SEND.

Repeat with four more former clients.

3. Initiate "Sell By Chat" with Five Clients on Facebook

"Conversations lead to conversions"—John Franklin, CMO of Two-Brain Business

Sell by Chat is simply a text conversation. Just as we once met our new clients at the ballfield and other social events, most people have 90% of their conversations through their phones now. So that's where we'll meet them.

If you have a public-facing Facebook group, that's the best place to start conversations. You can share good advice in the group; you can even start conversations with lead magnets; or you can simply start by engaging with people who respond to your public posts.

Let's start with the public posts.

Post something that asks a question.

For example, "What's your least favorite exercise to do at home?"

When people respond, send them a DM.

Start a conversation as if you were talking to them in the coffee line.

Ask them questions about themselves. If it feels like they'd be a good fit for your gym, invite them to try it.

You can also message the people who comment on your paid ads.

160 THE GOLDEN HOUR

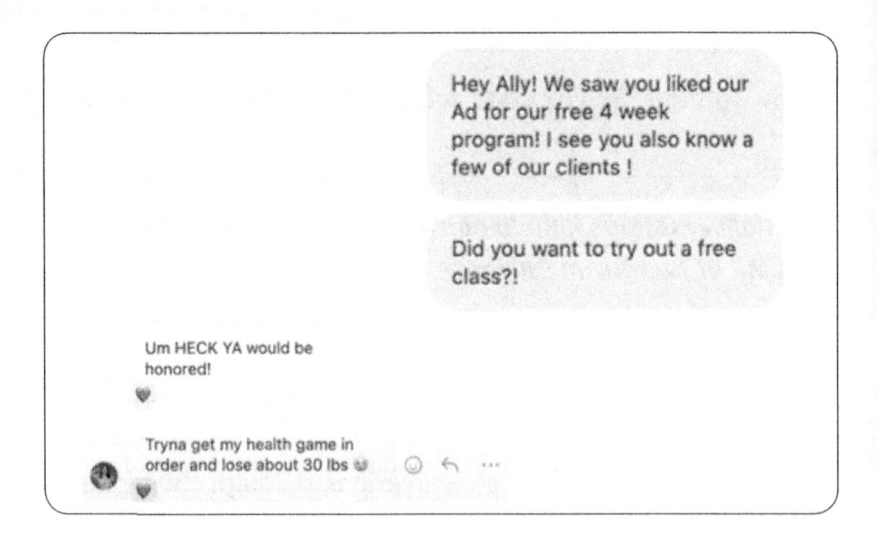

> Hey Ally! We saw you liked our Ad for our free 4 week program! I see you also know a few of our clients !
>
> Did you want to try out a free class?!

Um HECK YA would be honored!

Tryna get my health game in order and lose about 30 lbs

4. Text Five Leads Who Didn't Convert

If you open your CRM or your booking software, you're sure to find people who booked an NSI but didn't sign up.

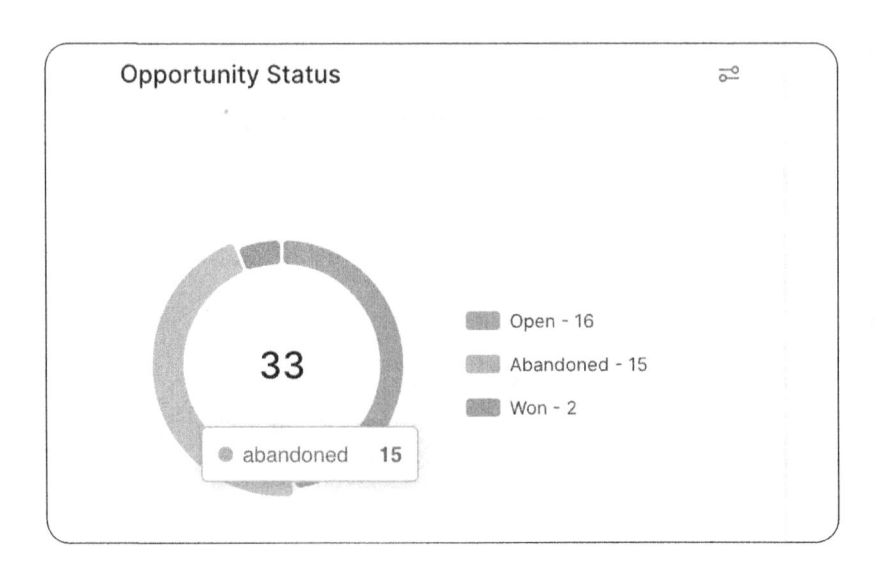

Opportunity Status

33

- Open - 16
- Abandoned - 15
- Won - 2

abandoned 15

Sometimes this was because they didn't understand your product, but most often it's simply because the timing wasn't right. 80% of the time, they didn't go join a different gym—they just didn't take any action to change their lives. It's our duty as coaches to reach out our hand and invite them to take action on their health.

Just start with "Hey [firstname]"

When they respond, we'd say:

> **Still interested in {offer}?**

If they're still not ready to sign up, I'd ask "What's holding you back?"

As you develop your sales skills, you'll get better at Sell by Chat—but it's never slimy or misleading, it's simply a caring coach asking questions to help them.

APPENDIX 5

HOW TO SET UP YOUR SOCIAL MEDIA CALENDAR

Our friends at Kilo walk you through this step by step:

Integrate

1. **Inside GLM, head to:**

   ▶ Settings
   ▶ Integrations

2. **Find the Social Media Integrations box and click 'connect. This will take you to a new window where you will need to log in with the relevant credentials and approve the connection.**

How to Set Up Your Social Media Calendar

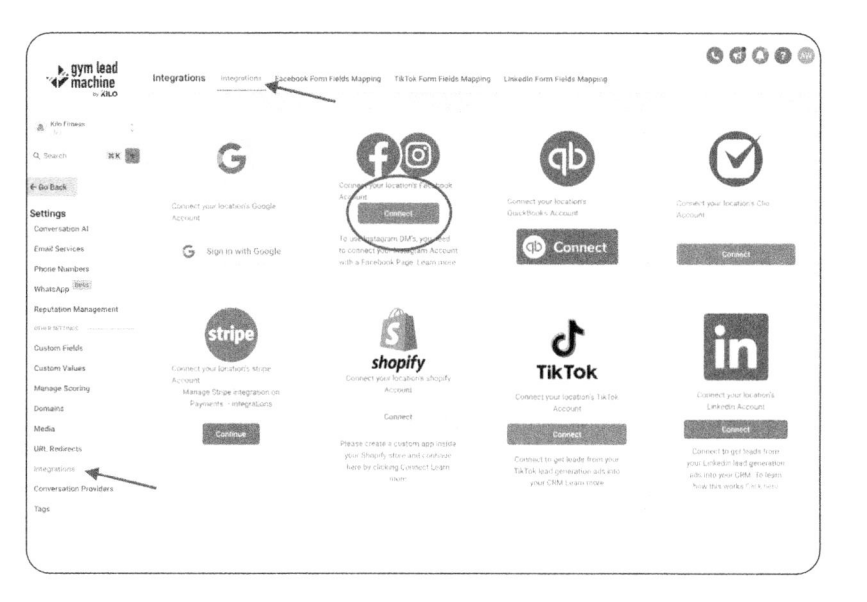

Connect the Social Planner

3. Back in GLM, go to:

   ► Marketing
   ► Social Planner

4. Select each Social Media Account and connect in turn. Once connected, you will be taken to the Social Planner dashboard.

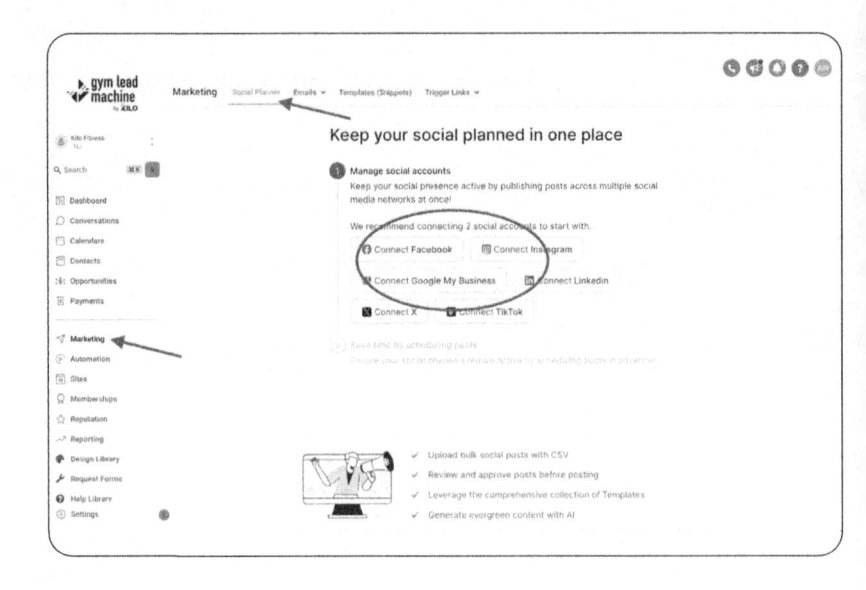

Make a Post

5. Click the blue 'New Post' button in the top right corner. Next, 'Create New Post'.

How to Set Up Your Social Media Calendar   165

6. **Next, use the drop-down menu to select the Social Media platforms you wish to post to. Use the check boxes to make your selection.**

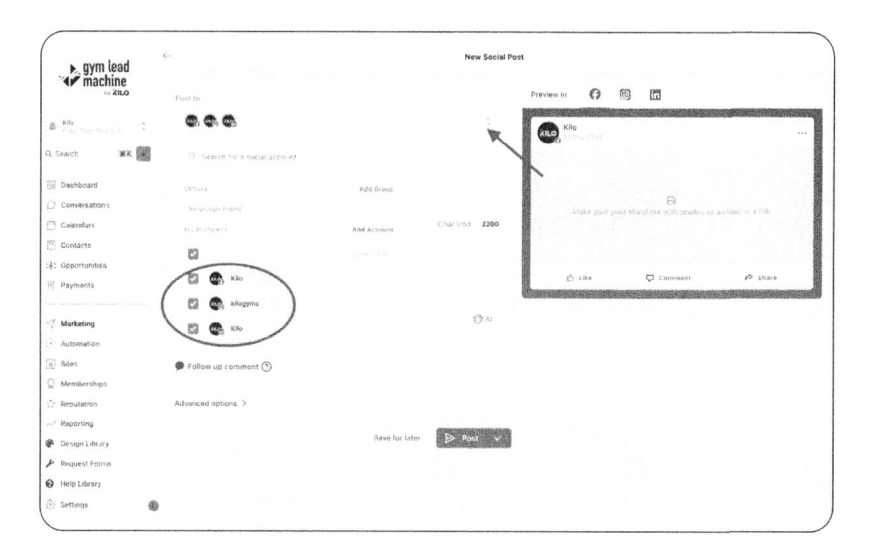

7. **Insert your copy into the text box.**

8. **Next, add your chosen image. Do this by clicking the little picture icon underneath the text box, and select 'Upload from Media Library'. Select your chosen image from the Media Library, or upload a new file.**

166   **THE GOLDEN HOUR**

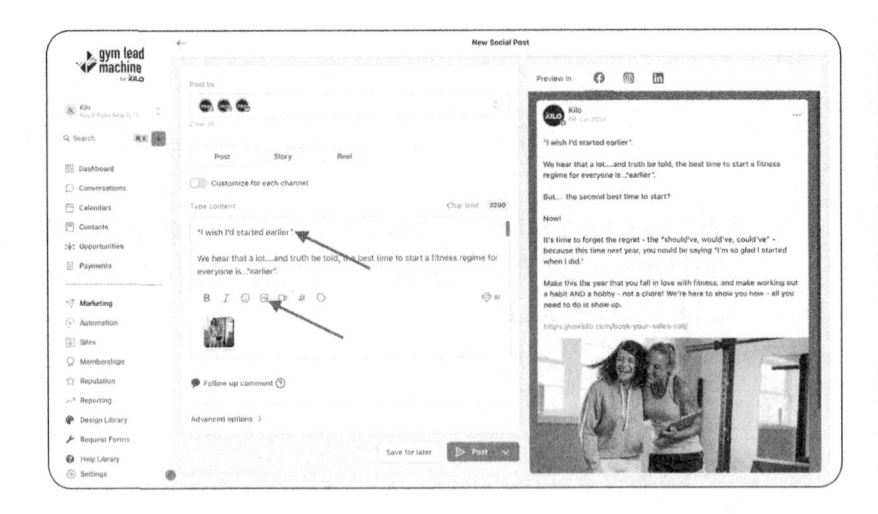

9. **Next, click the toggle on for 'Customize for each channel'. This will now allow you to customize the content (importantly, the format of the call to action) appropriately for each social media platform. You can preview each iteration of the post by clicking on the different platform icons.**

10. **We recommend the following for the key three platforms, each including a clear call to action:**

- **Facebook:** Add a clickable link
- **Instagram:** Refer to the link in the bio (ensuring that this contains a link to book)
- **Google Business Profile:** Add a call to action button with the relevant label (eg 'Book') and insert the link

11. **It's time to post / schedule! Click the blue 'Post' button if you want to post immediately, or click the arrow to select more options.**

12. **If you want to schedule the post(s) in the future, select 'Schedule Post'. This will take you through to a calendar where you can select the date and time.**

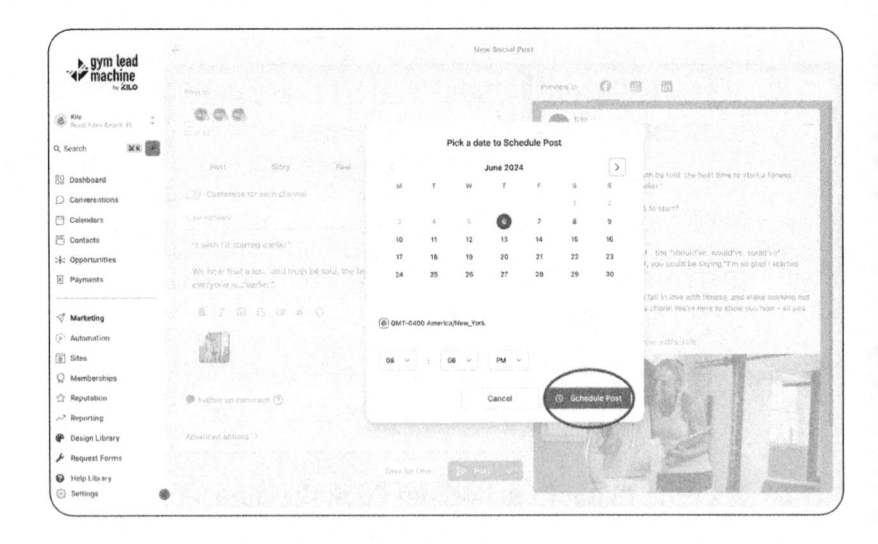

13. You will now find the scheduled post(s) on the Social Planner dashboard, under 'Scheduled Posts'. To make changes, click the three dots on the right hand side. Choose 'Edit' to adjust the posts, 'Clone' to duplicate the post (to allow scheduling for an additional date, or make changes to a copy of the post before scheduling), or 'Delete' to remove the scheduled post(s) completely.

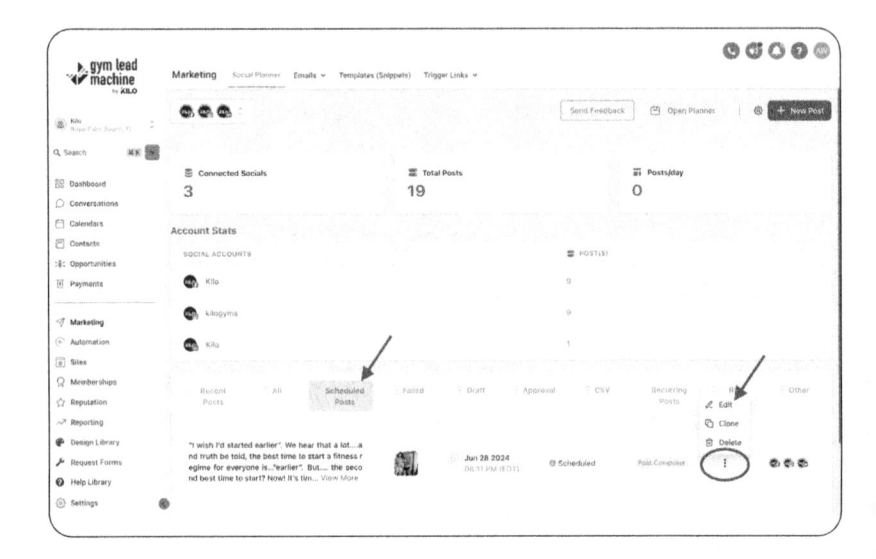

Connect An Additional Social Media Account

You can connect an additional Social Media Account at a later date if you wish—this is not limited to the first time you use the feature. To connect an additional account, click the icons in the top left corner of the Social Planner dashboard, and select 'Add Account'.

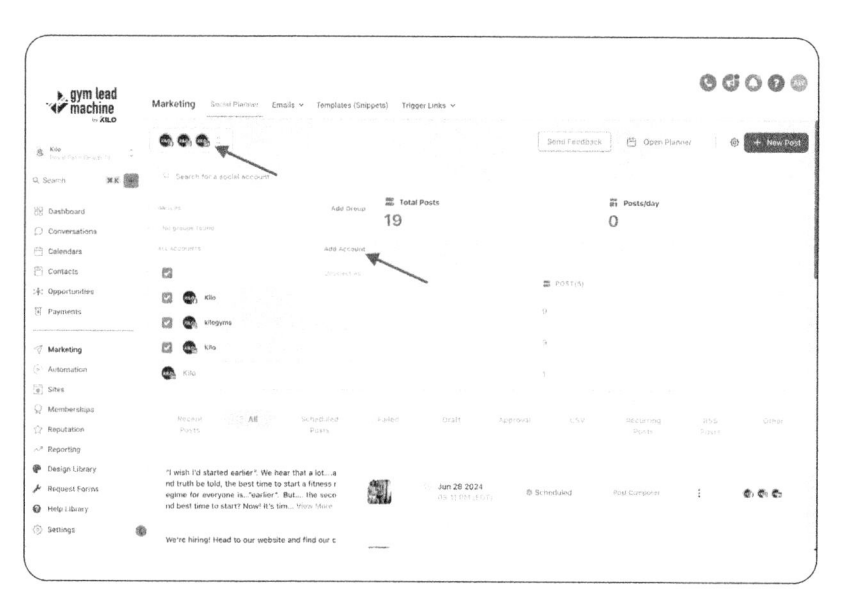

Calendar View

From the Social planner dashboard, select the light blue button in the top right corner labeled 'Open Planner' to see a Calendar view of your scheduled and historial posts.

From here, you can add a new post on a given day, by clicking the small blue '+' button on that day.

You can also find the same Edit options for existing scheduled posts that you would find on the dashboard list view, by clicking the three dots on any scheduled post.

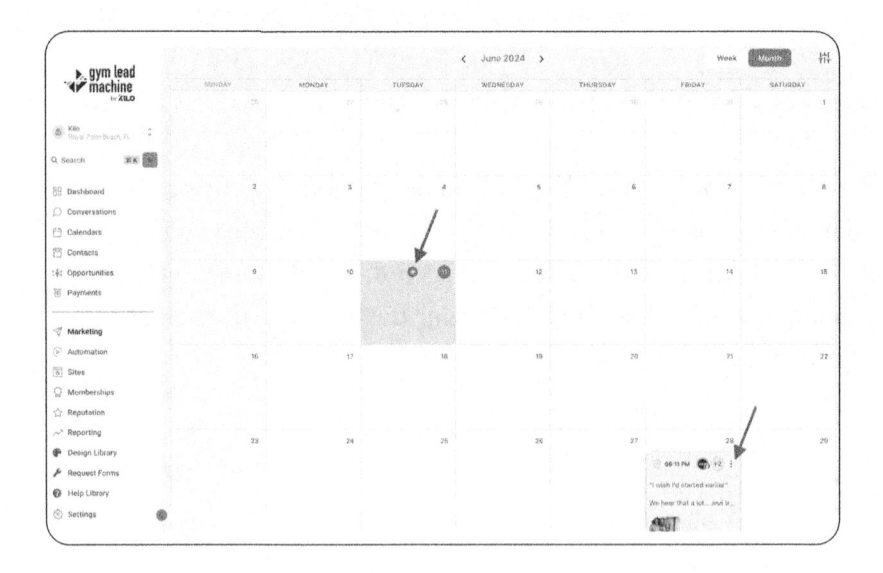

Finally, some social media platforms, like Facebook, allow you to set up your posts in advance. You can simply build the posts and schedule them.

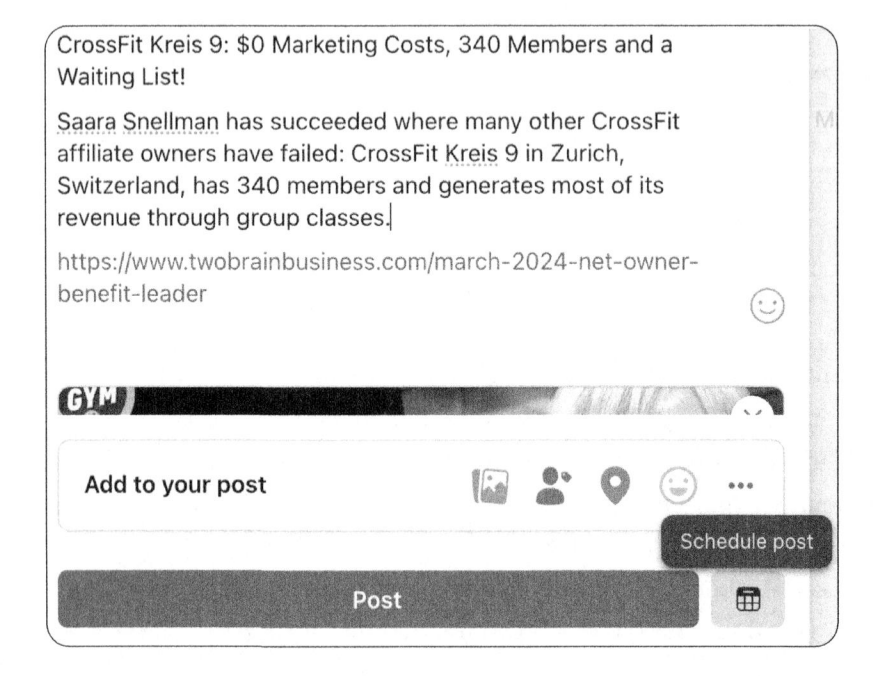

Then:

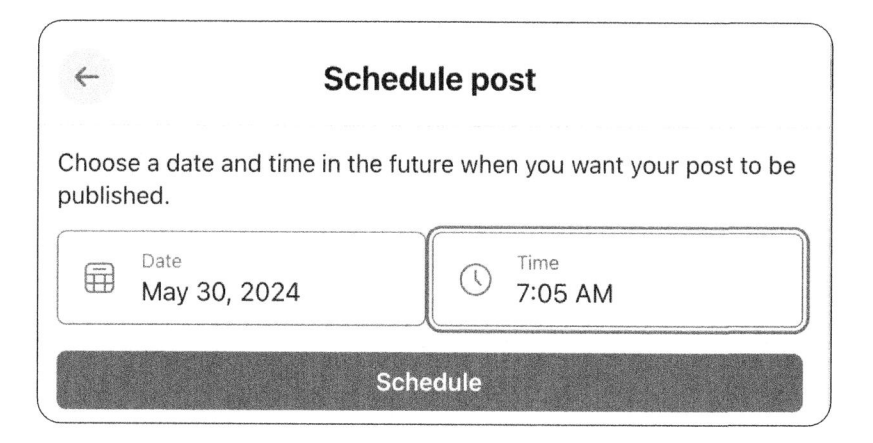

Schedule post

Choose a date and time in the future when you want your post to be published.

Date	Time
May 30, 2024	7:05 AM

Schedule

The point to having these done in advance is that it will make posting easy and fast next week. And then you can use the rest of your Golden Hour to work on larger projects, knowing that your base-level marketing is loaded and ready.

APPENDIX 6

HOW TO SPOTLIGHT YOUR CLIENTS

Saturday is usually a more relaxed day in your gym. With fewer classes on the schedule, and clients who aren't on their usually workweek timeline, the environment is less rushed.

Use the opportunity to take pictures. If you run one class on Saturdays, it's probably a larger one. Have your secondary coach take at least 10 pictures of the class in action—and always end the class with a group pic outside your gym.

You want pictures of smiling faces, not pictures of people collapsed everywhere. Put them in front of your logo. The simple rule is "Happy, not hardcore".

After class has finished, grab 1-2 clients and say:

"I'm so proud of you! Can I share your story on our social media?"

When they agree, pull out your phone. Ask them these 3 questions:

"What brought you to [your gym] in the first place?"

"What's your favorite part of [your gym]?"

And

"What advice would you give to the person you were a year ago?" (pick a date before they joined.)

These will be 3-5 minutes long, at most.

Have your staff upload the videos and pictures to a Google Drive folder, where you can use them on your website; on your social media Stories and Reels later.

Tag the person when they're posted so they can reshare.

This is not an imposition; most people want to be bragged about; and you have a platform that will make them feel famous.

If they don't want to do the interview, no problem—sometimes 1 person in 10 will decline. Just move on to the next.

If you can't find a client to interview, pick a staff person.

APPENDIX 7

HOW TO SEND A WEEKLY PREVIEW TO YOUR STAFF

This is 'internal marketing, and it's just as important as all of your other marketing. This is what keeps your staff excited about your gym and their place in it. Just as you have to sell strangers on fitness, and sell your clients on continuing to train with you, you have to sell your staff on the vision and the future. When staff run out of future at your gym, they'll quit to start their own, or quit to join the new gym down the street. And if all they hear from you is rules and operating procedures and evaluations, they won't feel as if they're being successful.

These 'weekly preview' messages are either a short post or a private QuickCast.

You can post in a private staff group on Facebook or Slack, or you can send a private voice message to your team (because it's much smaller than your client or public lists).

Here's the format:

1. A lesson you learned this week (ideally from one of them)
2. What's coming next week
3. Why you're excited about next week.

How to Send a Weekly Preview To Your Staff

My weekly preview to gym staff would look like this:

1. Here's a great tip I learned from Coach Jessica this week (this makes Jessica feel important and lets staff know you value them)
2. A quick preview of next week's group programming, and the intent of each workout (this works better than doing long lectures about aerobic vs anaerobic training, and helps them explain the workouts to your clients)
3. Something that's going really well in the gym OR something coming up that clients and staff will love.

Send this early Sunday morning. Keep it short, or it will be 'one more thing' for them to learn and remember. This should make their life easier, not be one more unpaid requirement of their job.

You can send this as a voice message through text or on Slack or on Facebook, or you can record a simple QuickCast just for your staff. You can also send as an email if you prefer.

Here's the RSS feed for my staff QuickCast. It's a walkthrough of the next week's programming, with the intention of every workout included, and one basic lesson from our blog.
https://feeds.captivate.fm/thecatalystmethod/
I also use a QuickCast for the Two-Brain mentor team. :)

Printed in Great Britain
by Amazon